WHAT OTH~~~ ~~~ ~~~~~ ~~~~~
MIKE AMATO AND THIS BOOK

"It was a pleasure to work with Mike Amato for over two decades and across two continents. Mike's sharp focus on culture was ahead of its time and in his book, *A Better Way to Win*, he takes the reader step by step through how to identify and build a winning culture in your organization. Not just another 'how to' business book, Mike keeps the reader fully engaged through his memorable analogies and life experiences gained through his inspiring leadership career. A book for serious cultural change agents."

– Deanna Oppenheimer, International Director and
Advisor, formerly Barclays Vice Chair-Global Retail Bank

"Mike Amato is like a ray of sun breaking through the skyscrapers of Wall Street. You'd be hard-pressed to find a finance executive who has invested more in people loving their jobs. From the stage he takes us into the corridors of finance where he's proven again and again that cultural transformation drives competitive advantage. If you've ever had to fight for a big swing in emotional momentum, if you've ever struggled to bolster morale when times are hard, if you've ever needed to prove that culture and ROI are intrinsically linked, then you should hear Mike Amato speak."

– Greg Larkin, former CIO, Bloomberg

"Looking for a better way to lead? Want to retain your best talent and create a culture that employees want to experience? Start here! Mike Amato is a brilliant business mind with an impressive track record for success, record-breaking profits, and creating organizational teams that come together to pursue a common mission and goal."
– Patrick Snow, Publishing Coach and International Best-Selling Author of *Creating Your Own Destiny* and *The Affluent Entrepreneur*

"There are many books about management and even more about leadership. But if you want to get to the very core of what it takes to move large, dysfunctional organizations into high-performance cultures, Mike Amato's remarkable story is a must read. He is the most passionate believer of putting people into the heart of everything, and he masterfully shares the key ingredients of successful transformation. This book is relevant, thoughtful, practical, and entertaining. If you are fighting for results, if you are struggling to create real momentum change, if you want to get to the bottom of corporate culture, or if you simply want to become a better leader yourself, Mike Amato's approach to free up the emotional energy in your workforce is an inspirational breath of fresh air. I have personally seen Mike Amato in action—he truly stands out in a banking industry heavily under fire."

— Dr. Olaf Theilmann, Partner, Deloitte, Former COO Barclays, Former CIO WestLB

"Mike Amato is a gifted leader. His experience in corporate America and international banking prove to be a solid foundation for this book. His ability to create strong culture in the workplace has definitely allowed him to show there actually is a 'Better Way to Win.' I highly recommend this book for anyone looking to step up their game."

– Kieran Murry, Author of *Go for Your Gold*

"What makes Mike special is the way he is able to effortlessly combine his intellectual horsepower with an incredible sense of empathy and connection with an audience, making the whole experience magical for all who get the privilege to hear him speak. It is nearly impossible not be inspired by his message, challenging all to see the world in an entirely new way!"

– Adrian Walcott, Managing Director, Brands With Values

"Mike's work inspired a proper transformation in my life. He's led me to grow as a human and professional every single day. From a professional perspective, I achieved measurable results in just two months. So again, thank you! Our sessions made a massive difference and have given me a roadmap and strategy for the rest of my life."

– Monica Millares, Head of Product Development at Big Pay in Kuala Lumpur

"Motivational, engaging, and memorable. That is Mike Amato. For more than twenty years, I have had the pleasure of observing Mike deliver countless public speaking engagements to massive audiences in multiple industries, across multiple countries, to multiple levels. The result is always the same. People leave motivated to be more, do more, give more. Mike engages the audience in every topic he presents because it feels like he understands–like he has been there. That's because he has. Mike knows how to connect with the audience, and he has an innate talent to use incredibly memorable analogies to keep it simple so everyone walks away with something they will never forget. Mike is outstanding, and his audiences will laugh, listen, and learn. I am forever grateful to have learned from the best."

– Erin Biertzer, Former COO,
Barclays Western Europe Retail Banking

"I met Mike in 2012 when he spoke at the Common Purpose – Leadership Without Authority event. Since then I have had the privilege of working with Mike as an executive coach. Mike has expanded my perspective and helped my business achieve results in a way that would have been impossible without him. This has enabled me to find myself, see my potential, and stretch toward higher goals.

I recommend Michael Amato to anyone who aspires to grow in their career and life, especially if they aspire to discover their potential."

– Berhe Woldu, Senior Finance Business
Partner at The Challenge

"Mike, I am sure you are being deluged with thousands of emails from your many dedicated followers. I count myself among that group. When people ask me about you, I call you the heart and soul of the retail bank. They say no one man makes a culture, but I think in this case they are wrong because your unique connection to so many employees is genuinely inspiring to me."
— John Benevento, Senior Group Vice President, Washington Mutual, New York

"It is clear you have the ability to motivate all employees to desire to make Washington Mutual the best company it can be."
— Dan Levin, Washington Mutual Employee

"Mike's natural ability to cut through ambiguity, define a clear vision, and communicate a strategy for success is compelling and powerful. Mike is a trailblazer, a mentor, and a coach, and he energizes people through his insightfulness and engaging personality. Thank you for all the learning and support."
— Nora Roberts, Head of Transition, Operations at Pay.uk

"Looking forward to this Mike. You were one of the most charismatic and inspirational leaders I had the privilege to work under in twenty-five years at Barclays so I know you have a lot to share with people."
— Mike Hutton, Director, Base 8 Communications

"From the first time I met you, I knew I liked you. You made everyone feel special and came across very sincere. I remember saying to you that my ship finally came in! It was you who created that great Wamu experience. I truly enjoyed working with you at Wamu!"

– Lynn Rossi, former Regional Director,
Washington Mutual Bank

"You were always such an inspirational speaker and a caring leader! You taught us no matter how busy we may think we are, manage the talent pipeline by building our bench strength as well as to understand the responsibility that goes with touching our customers' financial lives! What a lasting impression this truly makes!"

– Valerie McKiernan-Castro, Branch Manager, Chase Bank

"Culture is the critical enabler of a company's ability to deliver sustainable profits. Left unchecked, an unhealthy culture dilutes long-term profits and can destroy even the best of brands. Having served on Mike's executive team during the journey outlined in his book, The Better Way to Win, I can attest to the incredible journey that Mike describes, witnessing the transformation of my own team firsthand. I have since applied the same philosophies in my other global leadership roles with great success. This book is an amazing resource for any leader looking to reshape the way they do business for the benefit of all stakeholders! Mike shows us how to transform culture at scale to create engaged teams, positive customer outcomes, and long-term shareholder value!"

– Bret Packard, Founder and CEO of
The Packard Network

"Combining an intense focus on employee engagement with true customer care and having the management support to drive such an agenda took us to an amazingly different place and created an energized, positive, and productive environment for employees that was felt by the customers. It was an approach that the unions and regulators couldn't help but get on board with. With Mike's unrelenting drive and ability to get 'the right people on the bus', I was able to be a part of a transformation many had a hard time imagining could ever occur, let alone believe how quickly it happened. So many leaders talk about advocating for customers and colleagues, and for most it's lip service. Mike actually lives and breathes it. He's one of the best examples that if you singularly manage 'to' profits, you will see more success than you could imagine."

– Robert Bond, former EVP, Heading up the National Branch Network and Chief Customer Officer

"After the Dime/WaMu merger, I was the one fortunate enough to show Mike around NYC. I could tell right away this was a person of incredible warmth and character. Later that day, Mike met the entire NY leadership team and reassured us about our future and place on the WaMu team. This one great man erased any concerns we may have had and made us all feel like a million dollars. We will never forget this moment or how privileged we were to have him as a leader, mentor, and friend!"

– John Jones, former Regional Director, Washington Mutual

THE BETTER WAY
TO WIN

Leading In a Time of Crisis

AVIVA
PUBLISHING
NEW YORK

MIKE AMATO

THE BETTER WAY TO WIN
Leading In a Time of Crisis

Aviva Publishing
Lake Placid, NY
(518) 523-1320
www.AvivaPubs.com

Mike Amato
(425) 922-8086
Mikeamato@amatosparks.com
AmatoSparks.com

ISBN: 978-1-636181-89-9
Library of Congress: 2022906323
Editor: Sara Stibitz
Cover Design and Interior Layout: Fusion Creative Works

Every attempt has been made to source all quotes properly.
Printed in the United States of America
First Edition
2 4 6 8 10 12

DEDICATION

I dedicate this book first and foremost to my wife, Rumi. Her limitless support, encouragement, and tireless patience during the writing fueled my desire to slog through even the tough times.

I also dedicate this book to my children, Becca and Tony. You put up with many relocations, new schools, new homes, and friendships while I pursued my career. The goal wasn't just to feed the family and climb the corporate ladder; it was always about doing something that would make you both proud of me.

To Deanna Oppenheimer, even though my methods were different and sometimes challenging, you believed in me and were the "air force" that kept the wolves at bay when times were scary tough. Without you, I fear all would have been lost. Thank you for your confidence that there was, indeed, a better way to win, allowing me to lead with confidence and courage.

To Jack Cornick, you taught me that living one's values is one of life's non-negotiables. And the wisdom you shared, with impeccable judgment, and a healthy dose of fun, helped me immensely as "What would Jack do?" became a favorite phrase of mine.

To Michael Towers, you had unreasonable confidence in me in the earliest stages of my career and showed me the motivational power of a leader's vision. Not only vision for shaping a high-performing culture, but vision that allowed me to see beyond any self-imposed limitations for my career.

There are many others who contributed to the stories in this book, but I'm certain it would not have been written without meeting Greg Larkin on the ride to Vienna from Graz, who then introduced me to my coach, Jason Connell, who then introduced me to my writing resource (whose patience was no doubt tested, maybe even shattered), Sara Stibitz. Working with Sara and Matthew Turner made this book possible. I also want to thank Patrick Snow for stepping in and helping me finalize the myriad of details needed to tie everything together.

Most of all, I dedicate this book to you, the reader. May my message on leadership and culture be an inspiration to you and your organization so that you too may discover a better way to win within your company and your career. If you will make your organizations better places to work, and better places to do business with as a customer, you, too, will see the benefits in all aspects of your performance, including exceeding shareholder and investor objectives. And that will make the world a better place for many thousands of employees and customers.

ACKNOWLEDGMENTS

I would like to extend a special thank you to the following friends, associates, mentors, and those who helped me make this book possible. This list is far from complete, but each of these individuals was impactful in the various stages of my career, so I've listed them alphabetically:

Alison Ramsden	Gwynn Virostek	Mike Miller
Brad Davis	Jack Cornick	Nic Parmakzesian
Bret Packard	Jan Schrag	Olaf Theilmann
Catherine French	John Benevento	Philippa Murray
Charlie Rozes	John Woodworth	Raefe Winstanley
Cindy Doty	Karen Richards	Ralph Coates
Dave Jeppesen	Ken Kido	Randy Grimm
Deanna Oppenheimer	Randy Grimm	Robert Bond
Debbie Bedwell	Ken Leander	Sandy Cavanaugh
Dick Wisenburg	Kim Kahmer	Sara Moorehead
Doug Springer	Kristen Bond	Sean Rowles
Drew Wolff	Larry Andrews	Stephanie Watts
Dyan Beito	Larry Bond	Steve Cooper
Elisabetta Osta	Lloyd Goodlett	Steven McGrory
Erin Biertzer	Mark Parsons	Tony Manisco
Gary Duggan	Matt Hammerstein	Vivek Ram
George Kaye	Michael Towers	

CONTENTS

PREFACE

A NOTE TO THE READER

"Culture is to recruiting as product is to marketing."
– Hubspot's Culture Code

The content of this book is intuitively known and felt by most who work in the rank and file of an organization, yet it typically escapes the notice of the organization's leaders in their relentless pursuit of ever-increasing shareholder return.

This myopic obsession with profit destroys the fabric of the organization's ecosystem by separating those at the top from the rest of the organization. This division appears when the stated values of the organization diverge from the values displayed and experienced every day. At best, this is the foundation for an underperforming organization. At worst, this is the cause of toxicity and dysfunction—an erosion of the very ecosystem meant to deliver value to all constituents who are impacted by the performance of the organization. We can't forget the various constituents or stakeholders while trying to please the shareholders.

When this dysfunction is allowed to exist, the fixation on shareholder return begins to *damage* shareholder return. The *art* of balancing the needs of all stakeholders for their collective good is replaced by the *science* of management through measurement.

"Know your numbers" dominates "Know your people."

"Know your customer" is replaced by "Know their data."

This is not new, and there are countless examples to cite over many decades—every week brings new examples of organizations in crisis because they lost their way. Rather than discussing various theories on the impact of healthy cultures, this book focuses on my firsthand experience leading a large organization mired in crisis and how we transformed the culture and saw dramatic results. Using my experience as a frame of reference, I'll share the recipe for turning dysfunctional cultures into incredibly high-performing organizations that deliver increased performance across all dimensions and to all constituents by engaging the entire organization.

Throughout my career, I have been fortunate to work for many tremendously supportive and patient leaders, as well as with tens of thousands of talented colleagues—many of whom helped me develop the philosophies shared in this book. However, I will avoid mentioning any by name. This makes me a bit sad, yet I do it for a couple of reasons. Primarily, once I start naming names in each of the stories I share, I am afraid I will invariably leave someone out. Secondly, this book would be twice as long if I attempted to fill the pages with my admiration and gratitude to every person who helped write this story.

One note that I wanted to share is that I am not a big fan of including exercises or discussion questions in books as I often don't have the time to complete them. Therefore, if you are like me and short on time, I give you my permission to skip past the reflective questions offered in this book. However, it you want to take a deeper dive to better understand the dysfunction in your company, then perhaps you and your peers may benefit from these exercises and use them as a catalyst to get to the core of the deep-rooted issues that may be holding your organization back. Use your answers to my questions to ultimately find your "better way to win!"

This book is written for those at the top of organizations who are interested in understanding the ROI of a healthy, functional ecosystem. It's also written for all of you who may feel stifled, underprepared, or underappreciated by your organization.

There is a better way to win. And I will prove it!

INTRODUCTION

THE POWER EQUATION HAS CHANGED

"The ones crazy enough to think they can
change the world are the ones who do."
– Steve Jobs

The power equation in companies, large and small, has shifted. While the leaders are continuing to sleep-walk their way through another rote speech on their tremendous culture and the value they place on their most valued resource, employees, workers are leaving for greener pastures in record numbers. The sense of entitlement that leaders traditionally feel about their workforce must be abolished and replaced by a new understanding that management is no longer a control function. Without this awareness, they can forget about trying to improve employee engagement scores (that had decreased between 2000 and 2019, *pre-pandemic*), and are fooling themselves if they don't take the time to understand how the relationship between executive leadership and the rank and file has grown more divided than ever before.

So, what's going on? How do all layers of management, from the board to executives to senior managers and on to middle and entry level managers not see the need to fundamentally change the way they do their jobs? It's well known that employees don't quit companies, they quit their boss, but how can a boss be more effective....more relevant...when they are being pushed from the top to do the same things to drive higher performance, just harder and faster, with less resources and smaller budgets, while their employees are demanding a greater connection and an employee value proposition that reflects what is in it for *them*? And what happens when these deep fissures are ignored or worse, expanded due to the ever-increasing pressure to produce results?

As you will read in this book, I lived this firsthand as a new executive in a company trapped in the vicious cycle that led to scandal as the dirty laundry was exposed on national TV. The subsequent crisis revealed the need to fundamentally overhaul everything we thought we knew about leadership, employee engagement, performance management, the definition of culture, and the necessity to deliver on obligations to all of those who depend on the business, not just the shareholders. I will share with you these dramatic, even stunning, results that drive my conviction that it's the focus on people over profits that ironically drives higher profits... and dramatic performance improvements in every aspect of the business.

By changing the traditional perspective of conventional wisdom, you will walk with me along my journey leading a large organization of 30,000 colleagues from crisis to prosperity, learning:

- How the myopic focus on profitability ironically damages profitability and begins to corrupt your workplace environment
- How to spot the early signs of cultural degradation before crisis strikes
- How the traditional approach to performance management smothers accountability, creativity, and ultimately, performance
- How the P&L of People and Leadership are the twin keys to unlocking stellar financial performance
- How shifting the organizational mindset from a survival mode to a creative mode increases employee engagement and delivers aspirational results
- How to structure the creation of an intentional culture using a framework that's effective for your entire organization, a division, or even a small team that is united in serving the common purpose, rather than their boss, and lastly,
- How to sustain your intentional culture by streamlining communications to end virtue signaling or moral grandstanding and connect with the organization on an entirely new, and deeper level

By applying these principles, you will see that inspirational leadership delivers better results, while changing the mindset of the organization and energizes the brand in ways that touch your customers.

My goal for you, whether you are a manager or an individual contributor; whether your company is flying high or struggling; whether you are new in role; or if you've been in your role for a long time and are seeing performance begin to drift, is that you avoid the pain of a crisis enveloping your organization by acting now. Using the experiences and underlying philosophies I share in this book, you will be able to create and sustain a healthy, high-performing organization with highly engaged employees, delivering your brand promise, by tapping into their discretionary energy.

This book is written from my perspectives that were developed from my personal experiences, observation, and philosophies from a career spanning forty years that began with me as a temporary employee at Washington Mutual Bank, answering the phone, then moving through the various layers of management, to become co-president twenty-four years later. As the values of that organization began to reshape its culture, I resigned and relocated to London to work at Barclays Bank as an executive responsible for all customer-facing and product areas with a team of more than 30,000 colleagues. Following the successful transformation of that organization from crisis to global leader, I joined the board of two banks in London as an independent director.

This career journey embedded a deep appreciation—perhaps obsession—for what it takes to attract, expand, and retain customer relationships, as well as my love and respect for the people who serve them. These are the people I served, and in so doing, I experienced the alchemy that resulted from my colleagues bringing their discretionary energy to work every day, united in the common purpose of delighting our customers. The focus on creating a culture that supported their growth to a high-performing team resulted in measurable improvements in every metric, from customer loyalty scores, employee engagement scores, productivity measures, and risk management lead to substantially higher profitability. I share these experiences with you not to attempt to impress you in any way, but to let you know that I have learned over many years what leadership methods actually work when leading your team, and what does not! I have learned of a better way to win and am sharing it with you here and now so that you can avoid the heartache and turmoil that would otherwise await you. The experiences I share in this book served to reinforce my conviction that profitability is the outcome of performance management, not the input that so many leaders seem to believe today.

I understand that your pressures to perform are greater than ever before, especially in light of the disruption caused by the pandemic, and that you may be struggling to enjoy your job, or advance your career to levels that you deserve, but I am convinced that the principles laid out in this book are more important than ever, and you will see the same impact in team and your individual performance by looking at your business in a different light. In fact, the title of this book is from an idea in an interview I heard one time by Pete Carroll, head coach of the Seattle Seahawks. Pete's leadership style is noticeably different than almost every other head coach in the NFL, and when he was asked how he attracts free agents to his team, he said, "I tell them there is a 'different way to win.' Not everybody has to do the same things to succeed, and we do things differently here…proudly differently." To underscore this point, the Seahawks, under the ten years of Pete Carroll's leadership, have been the league's second-most-winningest team.

The challenge is that doing things differently can be an uphill battle, with resistance along the way. While almost no one would argue that being customer-centric is a key to business success, nor that engaged employees boost performance, it's shocking to me that many leaders, especially under pressure, devolve to managing profitability, rather than the ecosystem that creates profitability.

In gathering the information necessary to write this book, I spoke to many people about the wisdom gained by living through the transformation of my organization. The reaction from all was palpable. Those in leadership positions embraced the concepts fully, reporting that with the multigenerational workforce and the restrictions forced on them by the pandemic, they've never had a more difficult time retaining their employees, much less engaging them. And all the while, investor/shareholder expectations have only intensified. Many asked if this book would be relevant today and show how they can meet all these expectations, despite the challenges. The answer is absolutely, yes! I not only share the formula, but the philosophical underpinnings and context for each step.

Those individuals I spoke to who were not in management immediately identified the signs of dysfunction appearing in various stages in the companies they work for, sharing their stories to provide a backdrop to their emotional appeal for a workplace culture that helps them thrive. Their questions were typically centered around whether this book would call out the growing gap between bosses and workers, "telling it like it is" from their perspective. Again, the answer is yes. Ending the virtue signaling by leadership and treating employees like adults in all communications was a foundation of the successful transformation described in this book, which contributed mightily to increased satisfaction and, therefore, performance by my teams.

Are you ready to see that crisis is the greatest opportunity to redefine your organization's culture by reestablishing the relationship between the various layers of management and the workforce? Are you ready to see how to shift the organization from survival mode to creative, growing mode? Then read on and see that *every* expectation of an organization by *every* stakeholder can be exceeded, which is truly The Better Way To Win.

1

KNOWING THINGS NEED TO HAPPEN

"Customers will never love a company
until the employees love it first."
— Simon Sinek, author, *Start with Why*

I placed the report on the table and sat back with a smile. I could hardly believe the progress we'd made over the last eighteen months. I knew we could do what some people thought was impossible, but as optimistic as I was in this belief, not even I could have predicted results like this.

The report contained the latest results on the balanced scorecard. We had created the scorecard as a baseline to measure progress across all five key dimensions of performance. The part that had caught my eye was the latest results from our employee engagement survey. It showed we had moved engagement from a shocking low of 64 percent up to 92 percent in only a year and a half. The response rates from the 30,000 colleagues on my team had increased from 77 percent to more than 95 percent, which was completely unheard of for a bank in the United Kingdom and proved they felt a connection to our vision.

I had taken our group chairman on a tour of the local market, introducing him to the local branch managers and employees, so I was sitting in my hotel room, quite tired, but I was also incredibly energized and looking forward to waking up the next morning to do it all again.

And to think, all this began with a single phone call eighteen months prior. I had been working late one night and was about ready to go home when my cell phone rang.

"I'm a producer from the BBC," the voice on the other end had said. "We're featuring Barclays in a documentary we're airing on Sunday on national TV." I smiled, excited to get a call from a world-famous broadcaster. Maybe they wanted a quote or to feature me on the show.

Excitement soon turned into panic as I frantically waved my boss into my office, trying to process what this producer was telling me. He said they had embedded reporters—posing as employees—in Barclays to secretly film an under-cover exposé. They were about to feature us on their show *Whistleblower*. I can still remember how I felt—my stomach churning and the palms of my hands sweaty. I couldn't comprehend what had just happened.

The BBC had placed three of their journalists in the organization nine months earlier because they suspected Barclays was mis-selling and treating its people poorly. They had se-cretly recorded everything and captured a lot of evidence to support the claim. They would release everything in forty-eight hours on the BBC.

I looked up to see my boss springing into action—activating the entire executive team, contacting the bank's attorneys, and notifying the group executive. This all seemed to happen in slow motion as I tried to gather my thoughts. Until that point, it had been just another late evening at the office, working as I had for the last few months, trying to turn around a business that had been seriously underperforming.

It hadn't been going all that well, but we were making some marginal progress. But then this phone call happened. This would change everything. A part of my mind was already planning my return to the States less than a year after moving to the UK.

Another part of me was angry. I was angry at the producer on the phone who had called with the news. I was angry at the previous leadership team for getting us into this mess in the first place. I was afraid that my time at Barclays would come to an end before making the impact I knew was possible. But more than anything, I was shocked.

My boss's initial reaction was the same as mine: "Is this even legal?" I was sure it wasn't legal in the US, but we later learned that it was perfectly legal in the UK. There was nothing we could do to stop them from broadcasting. We spoke with the producer, shared some choice words, and asked him why he had even called me if there was nothing we could do. "We thought you would like to know," he said. Well, I didn't want to know. All I could focus on was trying to stop the program while assessing what they would have uncovered during their undercover operation. But as my colleagues paced the room, called lawyers, and began trying to place blame, I tried to calm my thoughts.

We needed to think, not react. Although I didn't know what to expect from Sunday's program, I knew it would not be good. Yet, I knew deep down that whatever they would show, it would have to be—at least in part—accurate. I had had a feeling for a while that there was a toxic and dysfunctional culture inside the organization, but I couldn't put my finger on it. My leadership team was too attached to the current status quo to buy into a necessary culture overhaul. They couldn't see the truth because they didn't believe in an alternate reality. Their whole professional lives were based on experiences they had at other banks in the UK. There was no awareness that differentiation was possible, so they deemed this notion of a dysfunctional culture illogical and impossible.

Still, I had to take responsibility for that. I decided to do everything I could to make things right. If I were to go out, I'd go out on my best terms. I had lived the reality of a flourishing culture at my previous job and knew the tremendous ROI that came with it. I knew what to do, and I knew we could do it—if our entire executive team didn't get fired over the weekend, that is.

As I looked back on it eighteen months later, I couldn't have imagined how bad it would get before the stunning turnaround. As I sat in that hotel room, I looked at the latest financial performance report again and shook my head. "How did we pull this off?" I asked, smiling.

The group chairman couldn't believe the change either. He had been very challenging when the BBC program aired, so this was especially gratifying. "This is an entirely different company," he said to me as we drove between branches in Brighton. "The energy is different. I can't believe this is the same bank." And he was right—the change was palpable.

In a relatively short time, we had transformed not only employee engagement, but also improved customer advocacy, dramatically lowered costs, increased productivity, and significantly improved profitability. We never could have ever predicted these results in the aftermath of that phone call and the chaos that unraveled on that dreaded Sunday.

BARCLAYS' BLOODY SUNDAY

When the BBC show aired, it was worse than we could have imagined. We watched the episode together as a leadership team. It showed employees mis-selling products, toxic leadership practices, and an entire culture built around hitting targets no matter the cost. Our reactions varied from anger to shame, and there were a lot of defensive people in the room. Once again, I had a lot of mixed feelings.

Part of me was frustrated because the journalism was very poor, if not incompetent and misleading. They spliced clips together to connect things that happened at different times and in different contexts, creating biased and flawed conclusions.

I also felt afraid. We'd already started to have conversations with the board, and I could feel the sniper's infrared dot on my forehead. Still new to the job, I feared I'd soon be back on a plane to the States.

Most of all, I felt a sense of responsibility. As much as I hated the reporting, the BBC was right. They had recorded terrible practices, exposed incompetent leadership, and unearthed a toxic, dysfunctional culture of which I was now a part.

Change often needs a moment of catalyst, and this program was an extreme example. We would either change or carry on as usual and have yet another new leadership team come in to resolve the problem. I decided to ensure we committed to change. If I were to leave—forced or otherwise—I'd leave nothing on the table.

The following days were chaotic as we spoke to different stakeholders. I sat down with my boss and had long conversations about the broken culture. We couldn't fix it with anything less than a complete overhaul. I'm grateful to her for not only agreeing but giving me the freedom and support to take ownership of the situation. Still, I faced several obstacles, especially from the group executive board that wanted to see a plan of action and immediate progress. They supported our ideas, but there was an element of doubt among most of them. They were looking for someone to blame, and my role and ideas placed me in the firing line.

"Why do you think these problems are systemic? Isn't it possible that you just need to fire the right people and get on with things?" one of the executives asked. "What exactly do you mean by culture? And why should we believe that you are the person who's going to fix it?"

These questions shook me. I knew what we needed to do, but this challenged me to organize my thoughts and clearly lay out the actions we needed to take. Trying to define culture and the fundamental impact it had was difficult. Everybody thinks they know what culture is, but few actually understand it.

To show them that I could lead the change, I had to delve into my past and explain my experience at Washington Mutual.

WASHINGTON MUTUAL BANK: THE RISE AND FALL

Back in the early eighties, I wasn't looking to get into banking. But in 1982, Washington Mutual, a small regional thrift in Seattle, rolled out a concept that was new at the time—Telephone Banking. Fresh out of university, I took a temporary job that paid me $7.50 per hour—answering phones. Twenty-four years later, I would become the co-president.

Over the first few years, I moved into the investment subsidiary and went from financial advisor to regional director. It all led me to work directly for the president of the investment subsidiary, which gave me unique interaction and insight with the parent bank. Unlike the investment division, the parent bank was anticipating incredible growth. I learned a lot during this time and saw how the parent bank was on a successful trajectory. So, when an opportunity to become the manager of the bank's largest branch came around, I took it—even though it was a step or two down the organizational ladder. This gave me a front-row seat to the creation of one of the strongest and most distinctive cultures in financial services—or any industry, for that matter.

Everyone else thought I was crazy to move from the executive team of the subsidiary to managing a branch—especially this branch. One manager called it the biggest rat's nest in the system, which is why nobody else wanted it. The branch underperformed year after year, yet I saw it as a chance to prove to my bosses that I had what it took. I loved the role, and I loved the people I managed. It didn't take long to turn the branch's fortunes around. When I took on the role in May, we were at the bottom of the league tables. By the end of the year, we had risen to second place, narrowly missing the top spot. We then spent the next twelve months in first place as the most profitable branch in the entire system.

Other branch managers couldn't figure out how this had happened. In my mind, it was simple: Shift the focus of our management team to Purpose, Belief, and Talent. Everything we did, every action we took and decision we made, was to serve our customers—as they were our *purpose*. This can only happen if you have the right *people* who *believe* in the cause.

Despite doubt from staff members, we focused on hiring the best staff, hands-on training, and customer-first service. We didn't rely on the HR handbooks or what the other branches were doing—or even what my boss was telling me, which was to clean house and start over. We did it our way, and we built huge success on the back of it.

I didn't realize it at the time, but everything we did focused on the branch's culture and how we treated people. Every stakeholder was as important as the last. I didn't set out to achieve this; it just naturally happened. As the months went by, we saw more and more success, creating the confidence in this formula I would need going forward.

My career subsequently grew following this success. After eighteen months as bank manager, I became a regional manager, followed by a move to the senior leadership team. The bank began a series of acquisitions that would result in eight-fold growth over thirty months—from $10 billion in assets to over $80 billion in assets. Each time we acquired a new bank, I was tasked with welcoming the new team on board. I spoke about the culture we built and how we committed to hiring the best people so we could deliver exceptional service to our customers.

No other bank did this, which is why so many acquisitions failed to deliver the potential value. Our competitors focused on what was best for shareholders. They either bullied the newly acquired organization into their culture or allowed both cultures to co-exist, which created a chaotic mess with no well-defined set of values from which to create a single culture. Alternatively, we were committed to understanding our customers and building a happy, productive, unified, and successful workplace. As a result, we rose to number one of all US banks for both customer advocacy and employee engagement.

We seemed to have figured it all out. I loved seeing so many happy faces excited about their roles. However, this attitude began to shift when the CEO brought in executives from places like Amazon, GE, and Chase. Slowly, the culture began to regress. We started taking on bits from each of the companies and, in the process, lost the most valuable cultural asset we had: a single, coherent set of values. When my boss—the president of the retail bank—left (and ended up at Barclays), she was replaced by someone who wished to fix something that wasn't broken. His exact words to me were that he would turn over stone after stone in the retail bank until he found something to fix. He would try to become the hero none of us needed. Never mind that we were coming off two years of over 35 percent net profit growth, and the mortgage bank—which he was brought in to fix— was on fire and falling apart.

The values had shifted away from being a fundamentally high-performing culture, intent on delighting customers, and instead focused on driving higher profits, regardless of the risks. Stock analysts had the run of the place, asking for more and more information on what we could do to increase the yields in our loan portfolios to increase revenue through subprime lending. Of the four constituents described in our value statement— Customers, Colleagues, Communities, and Capital Markets—only one still mattered. Capital Markets were now king.

I watched this change unfold. In meeting after meeting, we discussed how to drive the high-performing retail bank harder to offset the failures of the mortgage division. We were addicted to the high of chasing subprime lending—increased risks and compromised values be damned. (Read the book *The Big Short* if you want more context on this.)

The CEO had been previously admired for steering our growth and preserving our culture. But despite serious constraints with the business model—that depended on home prices increasing—he began to confuse his role of maximizing shareholder value with ensuring the bank remained independent from takeover. A merger or outright sale was the most prudent way forward, but that would have put his role and the bank's independence at risk. I'm oversimplifying a complex situation, but one year after being promoted to co-president of the retail bank (twenty-four years after I was hired to answer the phones), it was clear that my time at Washington Mutual had come to an end. I simply couldn't accept the rejection of the very values that had made us successful. I had watched a company grow against all odds into a national powerhouse on the strength of its culture. Then, I saw how it began to fall apart with the decline of that same culture. I made the rather difficult decision to leave and moved to the UK to work at Barclays.

Little did I know that within two years, Washington Mutual would be the biggest bank failure in US history—a tragic end for the institution my former colleagues and I had loved. The regional thrift with fifty-four branches and $3 billion in assets had grown to 2,100 branches and over $300 billion in assets (#6 in the US). But it had destroyed the culture that allowed it to thrive by allowing its values to shift. When people ask me about the ROI of culture, I can't think of a better example than WAMU.

This experience proved to be incredibly helpful during the unfolding crisis at Barclays, giving me unique insights into what it would take to redefine its relevance with its stakeholders.

THE MOMENT OF TRUTH

That fateful Sunday presented us with some hard facts, whether we were ready to acknowledge them or not. But that crisis turned out to be the greatest gift we could have possibly received. Without it, I'm not sure we would have convinced the entire organization that the culture needed to change. They wouldn't have believed that there was a better way to win. The temptation to repeat the same failed actions with greater intensity would have been too great to resist.

Regardless of the journalistic quality, the BBC captured mismanagement, mis-selling, and an underperforming organization that had lost its way. The problem was clear, but the root cause was not.

This is where my small team of change agents and I turned our attention as we tried to determine what the current culture was, compared to the culture we wanted to build. We had an opportunity to start fresh, but we couldn't do this until we knew the whole story. Once we started to dig, what we found was worse than I could have predicted. Even more frustrating, the warning signs had been there all along.

We had all seen these signs and tried to tackle them but hadn't really been able to move the needle. Any progress we made was incremental. The *Whistleblower* program showed that incremental wouldn't cut it. A complete overhaul was necessary. Even the biggest defenders of the status quo had to admit that a massive change was in order.

The first warning sign I noticed centered around our graduate intern program. My role at Barclays covered all product areas of the company (mortgages, personal loans, savings, current accounts, investments, etc.) and all channels (branches, telephone, and online) for consumer, premier, and local business. Some called us the people part of the business because, with nearly 30,000 employees, we represented over 75 percent of the employees in the company, and we served over fourteen million customers.

When I arrived, we had thirty-two graduate interns who had spent time in various parts of the organization over the past several months. At the end of their stint, which was just a few months after I started, only one of these decided to remain in the retail bank. The other thirty-one interns left to work in the commercial bank, credit cards, or the investment bank.

We were supposed to be the people part of Barclays, yet we couldn't retain the people we had already recruited and trained. I knew from my time at Washington Mutual that employee engagement is a huge part of a company's success and a key indicator of a strong, aligned culture. Barclays' employee engagement was nearly non-existent. This was a powerful indicator that we had serious flaws in our ecosystem that rendered us unattractive to the best and brightest talent.

Another red flag appeared in many of the meetings I was in. I noticed that there seemed to be an abundance of consultants from every division. Wherever I went, there they were. I recall one meeting I was in with six other people. Halfway through, I decided to ask who worked for Barclays. Only one person raised their hand. The other five were consultants.

We had developed a culture where managers and executives outsourced thinking, planning, and strategizing. Rather than taking ownership, we hired consultants to tell us what to do. That way, there was someone to prepare the recommendations, and they could be held accountable if the recommendations didn't work.

During these first weeks, I had never seen so many PowerPoint decks in my life. On my first day, after meeting with several members of my executive team, I had decks stacked on the floor as high as my desk. I was blown away by the executives' intelligence and their ability to articulate what their businesses were doing and how they performed, but I learned very quickly to turn to the last page of the deck and skip the many pages of buildup. We didn't have a team of leaders as much as we had a team of analysts.

This led me to my third realization: Our executive meetings were unpleasant. Each executive arrived armed for battle and represented their business or division rather than the whole company. Each executive focused on their own profit and loss. Working together had never been a value worth pursuing.

This divided nature, combined with a lack of ownership and identity, fueled a dysfunctional culture that had been destroying the underlying culture for a long time. The BBC captured this on camera, as they recorded embarrassing conversations and employees following questionable policies.

They showed a company that had misplaced its values and put profits before people. Déjà vu.

FROM THE BOTTOM TO THE TOP IN EIGHTEEN MONTHS

With all this behind me, that evening in the Brighton hotel room was a great time to reflect. Considering the massive progress we had made, I poured myself a glass of wine and looked out toward the sea. I could not pretend that the last year and a half had been easy. All our capabilities had been tested, and we worried that we faced an impossible task. However, we had fundamentally transformed the company's performance even while the financial crisis unfolded around us. The report in my hands showed remarkable improvements in all five dimensions of our scorecard, and we knew this was just the beginning.

Customer: We had moved from sixth in the country in customer advocacy to second. *We became the preferred choice for current account switching and savings.* Brand awareness climbed, and complaints dropped significantly.

Colleague: Employee engagement moved from 64 percent—the lowest number I had seen in any bank— *to 92 percent, which was 5 percent higher than the global high-performing norm.*

Management Effectiveness: We had increased efficiency by removing £250 million in costs, consolidated nearly 250 underperforming branches in overlapping markets, and improved productivity via sales per seller—*moving from below ten sales per week per seller to more than twenty-three sales per seller per week.*

Quality: *We had no failed audits*, down significantly from the five failures the year before. We launched welcome calls to over 13,000 customers to confirm the quality of the sales process. And, reflecting the regulator's concerns with Payment Protection Insurance, we were the first and only bank in the UK to voluntarily eliminate that product.

Financials: The improvement in sales and efficiency had catapulted us from just *48 percent to plan pre-crisis to 140 percent to plan* and resulted in several reforecasts to cover shortfalls in other divisions—which was new to the retail bank as, typically, the reverse had been true (other divisions had to cover our shortfall).

Yet the most dramatic change of all, and the one I'm most proud of, is something you cannot measure or place into a report. As we drove around Brighton that day, visiting branches and getting to know the employees who dealt with our most important people (the customers), I saw happy faces free from stress and concern, proudly sharing their numbers that they would have thought impossible pre-transformation.

Our managers felt supported. Their staff felt appreciated. The customers they served were getting the service they deserved. The chairman of the group noticed it, too. This is the true impact a positive culture—aligned and delivering on the core values—has on a business. You can measure the ROI of culture and track its progress over time, but the true meaning and its impact remain within the immeasurable aspects of a business. It's experienced, not analyzed. It's felt, not measured. It's the single aspect of a company that has an enormous impact on every other part of it.

This is because culture *is* the company; it's the soul, purpose, people, and golden thread that keeps everything intact. As with most powerful facets in life, it's often misunderstood by those who profess to know the most about it.

This is the backdrop of the journey we will take together in this book. It will reveal the power of culture—both the positive and the negative—and how to create an *intentional* culture that aligns with the company values and delivers far more than the brand promise. It shows that there is a better way to win.

REFLECTIVE EXERCISES

1. How would you describe the soul of your organization? Are you able to articulate its strengths and weaknesses?

_____

_____

_____

_____

_____

_____

2. How well does your description above match what the organization declares or desires? Are the promises embedded in the vision and mission statements being delivered?

_____

_____

_____

_____

_____

_____

_____

3. What are the potential risks if the gap between reality and the desired states grows too wide?

_____

_____

_____

_____

_____

_____

SUMMARY/KEY TAKEAWAYS

The crisis of having our brand trashed on national TV could have generated several responses and outcomes, but thankfully we chose to invest in the culture as the culprit, not a few sacrificial lambs. The fortunate experience I had prior to this crisis proved to be the magic potion: I knew what good looked like and the focus was on spreading this belief throughout the entire organization. The results stunned everyone, me included, but ratified my conviction that taking the time to connect with people (customers and colleagues) pays huge dividends, far beyond the results generated by simply ramping up the pressure to perform better, with the resulting success more sustainable and far-reaching by many magnitudes. As you think about your organization, it's important to be conscious of any perceived gaps and have a clear understanding of the risks posed by a culture that becomes off-track. One difficulty I see expressed by senior leaders is that executives don't always have the same sense of urgency around the dangers posed by a shift in the culture, or if they do, there seems to be a reluctance to act. We will discuss this in more detail in later chapters, but a number of factors conspire to create inaction by leaders. This is a growing challenge that must be addressed.

2

DEFINING CULTURE

"Culture eats strategy for breakfast."
– Peter Drucker

What is culture?

I can still clearly recall one of the Barclays executives asking me this question in a meeting. I felt like the question was simple and one that I could easily answer. I thought I knew well what culture was and its importance. I had experienced the impact it had at Washington Mutual. I had helped build the amazing culture that took us to the top, and I saw success crumble once we took the heart and soul out of the culture. I should have been able to write an entire book on company culture. Yet, when that executive asked me about it, I didn't quite know how to say it concisely.

I found defining culture somewhat difficult because it's one of the most misunderstood terms in business. Most people think they know what it means, yet vague definitions didn't work when we were to transform a dysfunctional culture into a functional one.

Most people think culture is the vision and mission statements and values that your leadership team discusses periodically at strategy retreats or briefly references in group presentations. Maybe it's a catchy tagline on your corporate website that tells the world what the organization stands for. Often, it's left until the last ten minutes of a long meeting—after the important topics like business performance, cost challenges, and budget shortfalls. While it may be something you talk about as a company and even share publicly in marketing campaigns, is it intentional? Does it align with the values and all aspects of performance management? Is it actively felt, experienced, and nourished every single day?

This is why that executive asked me the question. He only had a vague notion about why culture is so important and didn't fully understand that changing the culture at Barclays was the answer to recovering from the devastating scandal. He figured that it was just another internal public relations campaign—an obligatory inclusion in the recovery plan—and that our culture wasn't all that different from other UK banks at which he had worked.

In his mind, culture was just a slogan. He thought the solution was to focus on executing better, trying harder, being clearer on what we needed to do, and increasing accountability for poor performance. I referred to this approach as "whipping the sled dogs harder." Another phrase I heard was "let them know there's a new sheriff in town."

This mindset made me realize the task I had on my hands. I didn't just have to help change Barclays' culture; I had to first educate the entire business on the power of an authentic, aligned culture where our most important values are reflected in everything we do. This wasn't going to be an exercise in increasing discipline with grim determination. I set out to show them that we had to free our team to perform at higher levels. As unconventional as it seemed, this freedom would lead to the higher performance demanded of us. There was a better way to win.

The very essence of culture centers around people coming together and progressing toward a common purpose, which delivers on the corporate vision described in the mission statement. Culture and the brand promise are two sides of the same coin, as the brand is how the culture becomes apparent to the customer, and culture is how the brand is reflected to the employees. It's easy—and quite common—to forget the customer and start believing that the business exists to make a profit or drive shareholders' returns, but this focus has an erosive, toxic effect on the culture. Of course, it is necessary to be profitable and drive adequate shareholder returns or the business will fail, but the genesis of every business is to provide a product or service to a customer at a fair price in ways that meet or exceed their needs and expectations. Ironically, only companies that have forgotten this feel the need to shout to the world that they put customers at the heart of everything they do. True customer-centric cultures know that who they are is apparent in their propositions.

Culture is the environment, or the ecosystem, within the company that leaders create to align employees wi' common purpose. The idea of culture is misunder' when it's no longer a description of how things truly function and how time and resources are committed, but simply what the leadership declares it to be. If culture remains misunderstood, leadership cannot intentionally achieve what they want. Remember, you can't not have a culture. The question is whether you have the culture you intend or an accidental, unintentional one driven by virtue signaling rather than authenticity.

At Washington Mutual, as a branch manager, we transformed the entire culture in a matter of months and celebrated amazing, unexpected results. I saw that we didn't treat our customers as well as we could, and I saw an unhappy and unfulfilled workforce who stopped believing we could be the most successful branch in the system. We didn't set out to create a great culture. It was a natural consequence of focused attention to people, training, and customers' needs. Once we set the table, the pieces all fell into place. And no one was as surprised by our success as the longest-tenured employees who were convinced that nothing could ever change the branch performance. Every week, they had different reasons why the branch underperformed: the market wasn't growing, the customers had all the products they needed, the building was old, etc. But as the truths they swore by were proven to be myths, they became the biggest supporters of the new reality.

This approach paid dividends when I was sent to California to integrate three successive acquisitions, each one subsequently doubling the size of our organization. The approach, which was developed years earlier in my career at a branch of twenty-five employees, was refined and scaled to allow us to bring our brand to a massive new market in California—adding 500 branches along the way. The question at Barclays was how to do the same thing in a larger organization with over 2,000 branches and a staff of nearly 30,000 people. We couldn't just expect results to happen at Barclays. The scale was too big. We had to have a formalized approach to the cultural shift and be intentional about everything we did—and did not—do. Otherwise, any progress we made would vanish when we faced inevitable challenges.

We couldn't just paper over the cracks. We had to get the entire workforce on board, start from the beginning, and re-invent ourselves. Barclays needed to know why culture was important and, more importantly, what it meant.

We needed a rallying cry that would inspire everyone to embrace change and consciously sign up for a new way of doing things. I couldn't speak to each person individually and explain why culture was important. I couldn't rely on large numbers of colleagues from the home markets coming in to show how we did things and why we did them. I had to create a clear, simple message that got everyone on the same page—from the leadership team to those on the front line serving our customers.

It was overwhelming. We were in the middle of a crisis, and the business was performing woefully. Pressure was high for all of us during this period. I knew we had to get this right, and if I didn't properly communicate *why* culture was so important, the *how* would never make sense. I had to make those on the leadership team believe in this as much as I did and then get the other thousands of employees on the same page.

The key message was that culture isn't what you say you do, but rather what you do when nobody else is watching. The BBC unearthed this at Barclays. We said we stood for one thing but defied it in practice.

It's important to note that while I believed the BBC did a hack job on us—at times cutting and pasting different scenes from different meetings to create a picture of dysfunction that would garner an emotional reaction from viewers—the reality is that they accurately captured a culture that had drifted far away from the type we said we valued. We said we were a bank that cared about our people and our customers, but the truth was out there for everyone to see. We were not about people, neither those inside our business nor those we served. Our primary focus was on hitting the budget, achieving financial targets, and driving hard to improve performance—which, ironically, was exactly what damaged our ability to achieve those objectives.

Our challenge was to create a high-performing organization that honored our individual and shared values, based on principles that we held most closely. To do that, we had to change the entire ecosystem, beginning with the things we were doing as a management team that caused a disconnect from our staff and customers. These gaps created an flattering view of leadership amongst the employees. We led to eliminate any discrepancies between our stated values and our practiced values, aligning our brand promise with a functional, intentional culture.

I told my colleagues that if we wanted to become the bank we told everyone we were, we had to live by those standards every single day. From the top of the organization to the bottom, we had to walk the walk. No more empty promises. No more clever marketing slogans or new campaigns. If we wanted to escape the crisis in which we had put ourselves, we had to change the rules of the game, and then, most importantly, every single person in Barclays had to live by them.

People are the key ingredient to change. No matter the size of your company, it's your people that define its culture—what they do when nobody else is around and how they come together as a collective to drive your business forward. This resonated with everyone and became the rallying cry the organization desperately needed.

REFLECTIVE EXERCISES

1. What does culture mean to you? Could you explain it to others clearly and concisely?

_____

_____

_____

_____

_____

_____

2. What culture changes can you make in your organization to better retain your talented employees?

_____

_____

_____

_____

_____

_____

_____

3. What obstacles stand in your way preventing these changes from happening?

_____

_____

_____

_____

_____

_____

_____

_____

SUMMARY/KEY TAKEAWAYS

Having a common understanding of what culture is…and isn't…is an incredibly important step to take when considering transforming something so fundamental to how the organization operates. It's commonly misunderstood, and at times, any complaint about the organization may be chalked up to culture, but equally likely, a valid observation of a cultural shift can be dismissed too readily as being overly dramatic. Therefore, a clear, common definition of what culture is helps you navigate the issues more clearly.

When in doubt, remember that culture is the brand expressed internally, while brand is the culture expressed externally. This is a powerful insight. When an organization fails to deliver on its brand promise, the customer makes their feelings known through complaints or migrating to a competitor. The same holds true when an organization fails to deliver on its cultural promise to the colleagues. Feedback grows to complaints which grow to undesirable turnover or worse, litigation. A common definition is a logical first step in avoiding these pitfalls and in achieving the growth necessary to succeed.

3

THE COMPONENTS OF CULTURE

"We believe that it's really important to come up with
core values that you can commit to. And by commit,
we mean that you're willing to hire and fire based on them.
If you're willing to do that, you're well on your way to
building a company culture that is in line with the brand
you want to build."
– Tony Hsieh, CEO, Zappos

In the early days of a business, the focus on culture is less crucial. Yet, as a business grows and more people and layers become part of the equation, the more complex the culture becomes. Add in the input of an ever-growing number of investors, and it becomes very difficult to maintain the culture that aligned everyone to the common cause in the first place. It takes a conscious effort to keep everyone on the same page and pursue the standards for which the company purportedly stands.

With this in mind, here are the key components necessary to create a high-performing culture:

1. Purpose: The unifying force. Why are we here? What defines our relevance to our customers?

2. Values: Our moral compass that defines what we stand for. The authentic beliefs that guide and provide motivation for our attitudes and Behaviors.

3. Behaviors: The specific ways we behave and how we treat each other reflect and reinforce our Values.

4. Structure: The way we reflect the delivery of our Purpose through our organizational Structure, which ultimately drives Behaviors.

All the while, people—*your people*—are the golden thread that holds the culture together. Many academics who study corporate culture like to have *people* as part of the process, but it's too important to simply be a part of it. It's *people* who sit above everything else, dictating what does and does not happen based on a firm understanding of human motivation, performance, and behavioral change. Remember, it's important to be conscious of what you do, not what you say you do.

The more people who are a part of an organization, the harder it is to keep these four key components aligned. This is how Barclays found itself in the middle of a crisis. In efforts to drive higher profitability and better business performance, the leaders had unintentionally lost sight of Barclays' vision and values. Investment shrunk, and there was no long-term plan to improve the customer experience. As the management layers all strived to perform financially, leaders became less customer-centric and more directive. Behavior changed, and the entire structure that kept everyone accountable changed with it. That's the reality of managing people: If the purpose changes—intentionally or not—the waterfall of values, behaviors, and structure changes to reflect that purpose. It's human nature to adapt to survive.

We had front-line workers focused primarily on hitting their targets because of the pressure applied through the management layers. Missing sales targets could ultimately cost one their job, so the primary purpose became about delivering on plans. Everyone wanted to be rewarded and recognized for a job well done. Plus, they wanted to avoid the pain of performance improvement calls with their boss's boss.

Their managers wanted the same thing, as did *their* managers, and so on. Survival is our most ancient, fundamental need—when threatened with the pressure to conform, we will logically act in certain ways to survive. High-talented individuals with better options begin to leave for greener pastures, while employees with more limited options remain. This is the exact opposite of what a leader would want in terms of talent pipeline management. Some signs that the organization is decaying under survival mode are regrettable turnover exceeding the desired target, the inability to retain the best recruits, and poor sales practices. Therefore, the objective is to change the environment in order to change the outcomes.

REFLECTIVE EXERCISES

1. What is your level of attachment to the purpose/mission of your organization?

_____

_____

_____

_____

_____

2. To what degree do your personal values align with those of the organization?

_____

_____

_____

_____

_____

SUMMARY/KEY TAKEAWAYS

Once you understand the definition of culture, it's helpful to break down the components of culture so that one can measure the organization's effectiveness in each. These are its purpose, values, behaviors, and structure.

Articulating the purpose is crucial as it invites an emotional attachment to the direction the organization is going. The mission statement represents the reason why the organization exists. As we go about our jobs each day, it's easy to lose sight of why the organization was created in the first place. Yet, every day at work, we are signing up to help complete this mission. If you haven't been reminded of it for a while and if it doesn't at least partially inform your actions, then this is undoubtedly true for others in the organization. The values, whether spoken or not, are the basis of every decision and action within the organization. An intentional or conscious culture has a strong set of values that are evident in everything that is said and done. Behaviors are the logical outputs of how each employee interprets their direction. Frequently, organizations focus on behaviors as the root of both successes and failures; however, often behaviors are merely a reflection of how a person is responding to the signals they are receiving in their environment. Look to change these signals in order to change behaviors. Finally, the structure is the subsequent organization of personnel and activities necessary to deliver on the mission. Ideally, the structure reflects the organization of executive talent and their teams to deliver customer outcomes. Aligning these four components of culture is a huge step toward creating and sustaining a healthy ecosystem.

4

THE IMPORTANCE OF CULTURE

"We are not here to curse the darkness, but to
light the candle that can guide us through that
darkness to a safe and sane future."
– John Fitzgerald Kennedy

When JFK visited NASA for the first time in 1961, he introduced himself to a janitor who was mopping the floor.
When JFK asked him what he did at NASA, the janitor
replied, "I'm helping put a man on the moon."

NASA had a vision, a purpose. It had teams of people focused
on vastly different tasks. The culmination of its vision would
take years to come to fruition, but each day, every single
person involved had to turn up to work with a common
goal in mind. *We are going to put a man on the moon.* "We"
is the keyword here. It didn't matter who the man would be.
All that mattered was a common purpose. To achieve this,
they all had to be on the same page.

NASA built a strong, aligned culture during this time because those at the bottom of the hierarchy still *got it.* The
janitor knew what he was a part of. He may only have played

a small role, but it was an important role, nevertheless. He took pride in his job. He must have felt inspired by those around him.

This doesn't happen inside a dysfunctional company with a toxic culture. This only happens when everyone is pulling in the same direction and buys into the purpose. When the entire organization is focusing on the brand rather than the financial results, the soul of the company emerges. By making financial performance an output rather than an input, higher profitability is the result. This is when discretionary energy is unleashed— the energy generated by someone who *wants* to do something rather than someone who *must* do something—and with it comes higher performance across the board. The company takes on an entirely different energy, and the success that flows motivates everyone to do even more. Soulless companies exist, but if a company can lose its soul, it can find it again.

I saw this firsthand as we scaled this idea through the rest of Washington Mutual during an intense period of growth. We successfully integrated more than thirty acquisitions by focusing on creating a common culture. For the larger acquisitions, I was to be the first point of contact for the field leadership teams and explain our culture in large employee gatherings. These situations were nerve-wracking. I'd arrive with a stack of papers full of facts, data, and key metrics, which, of course, everyone expected me to present. As many as two hundred and fifty senior leaders, many of whom were about to lose their jobs, stared at me with their arms crossed. You could practically feel the resentment in the room.

So, I'd deliberately stand up after my introduction, set that big stack of paper down on my chair, and approach the stage with nothing in my hands. I'd turn off the video projector and stand there for a few seconds surveying the room. I'd then begin to speak, not about the usual business objectives, strategic overviews, targets, or facts, but about what Washington Mutual stood for and what we were trying to achieve. I was simply speaking as a person to a group of people, treating them as the adults they were. The focus was on our culture, the behaviors that we valued, and the customer needs we fulfilled. I conveyed my message in an informal way, delivered from the heart, and extended an invitation to the newly acquired organization to join our company if the values fit.

As I spoke more about our values and culture and how we did certain things, the mood in the room would visibly begin to change, arms came uncrossed, and curiosity replaced resentment. I'd go on in detail to explain our values and how important they were and how they showed up in the way we worked together—not just a marketing ploy, but actual values we live by each day. I described the strengths of this approach, as well as the opportunities for us to improve. I'd tell them if they didn't agree with these values, it was okay. I was merely inviting them to join what I believed in my heart was the highest-performing, most-human culture anywhere in the US at that time. I'd give them an option to leave before taking any further steps—no judgment, no pressure from me or anyone else. We were open to ideas and how to improve on the areas I had shared, and we wanted to work with them and bring them into our Washington Mutual family. But our core values were non-negotiable.

My exact words, which became an integral part of all our future indoctrinations to Washington Mutual, were, "Be happy and be here. Or be happy and find another organization that fits you better, if that's your choice. Just don't be here and be unhappy because this will be reflected in your performance, and you will force me to help you seek a career elsewhere, which I never like to do." I wished to challenge and engage them, to make them feel like they were a part of something special. The quiet confidence apparent in this phrase had an amazing effect on all attendees. After speaking for some time about our culture, I would open the floor to questions—many times answering them for hours. This confidence in our culture and authenticity was a welcome relief for almost every attendee, and you could see people were ready to sign up right then. It was intended to acknowledge and address their greatest fears about the upcoming integration and to give them an honest and direct view of who we were so that they could make the best choice for themselves. I also committed to transparency in the process of job consolidations—they would get the latest information on these decisions as soon as I had them.

This is possibly the greatest benefit of building an intentional, powerful, and positive culture. It draws a line in the sand that pulls the right people closer and pushes the wrong people farther away. It's a polarizing line that says we stand for something important. Those who fit want to be a part of it. Those who don't won't. The result of these sessions was that the contribution of our new colleagues strengthened our culture rather than diluted it. Dilution of the culture is typical for acquisitions and a primary reason that most don't work out as planned.

It creates a journey. Not everyone will want to be a part of it, but those who do can clearly see what stands before them. It's this journey that roots your people to those key components: *purpose, values, behaviors,* and *structure.* If you give your people a journey worth being on, you will build a culture that thrives.

REFLECTIVE EXERCISES

1. What is the happiness index inside your organization?

_____

_____

_____

_____

_____

_____

_____

2. When people at your company express unhappiness, what is that makes them feel that way?

_____

_____

_____

_____

_____

SUMMARY/KEY TAKEAWAY

The courage of leadership is funded by the confidence in their ability to recruit the best and the brightest. There are a lot of things that go into this statement, such as the ability to define the type of talent needed, the aspiration to have "the best person in the world at every job," the ability to fill key roles from within, i.e., internal recruiting, and a culture that attracts, enables, and encourages high performance. But it's the leadership's ability to articulate what the organization stands for and how this comes to life in the way the organization is run that sets the stage for this type of leadership confidence.

It's always interesting to watch the reaction from leaders about the question on happiness. Usually, a quick affirmative response is accompanied by a somewhat confused look in their eyes. Most people have never thought of "happy" emotions coexisting with something referred to as "work." But this question is intended to give you something to ponder and assess. And, yes, happiness is a crucial aspect of how we spend one-third or more of our lives.

Equally important is to begin to understand what causes people in your organization to become unhappy. While it's impossible to always be filled with joy at work for any number of reasons, understanding those things that create unhappiness provides insight into how deeply they are affecting employee engagement, the underlying culture. And subsequently, performance. Is it the policies that create unease? Is it personalities? Or is it the direction the company or a leader is travelling? Each of these has different consequences and requires different levels of response. Like so many things in life, awareness is key.

5

THE SOUL OF A COMPANY

"Corporate culture is the only sustainable
competitive advantage that is completely within
the control of the entrepreneur."
– David Cummings, Co-Founder, Pardot

When you have an intentional, high-performing culture,
you'll notice your company has a soul. The soul of a company is the feeling, the vibration, the energy one can sense
when speaking to employees and managers of that company.
Conversely, I have heard time and time again of workers
complaining that their company's sole focus on the bottom
line has killed its soul. They complain of feeling disconnected from the very reasons that caused them to join that
company in the first place. But does the soul of a company
matter? And how can a focus on profits, which is surely a
primary objective of the company, have a detrimental effect
on culture?

When a company finds its soul, the collective group is unified by the purpose. These employees are engaged in their
work, supporting the vision which attracts their discretion-

ary energy. They do more than required because they want to, not because they must. They are excited about their prospects personally and professionally. Of course, there are still personality clashes, politics, good guys, and bad guys; but as a whole, the organization is performing at a high level, sometimes well beyond the benchmark. The result—as I've said many times before—is that profits soar. The mentality of hitting targets and budgeting is replaced by an attitude of hitting stretch goals and innovation.

Ah, innovation. That elusive trait every CEO craves. Creating an environment where innovation thrives and is incredibly desirable, yet difficult, especially for larger organizations. Innovation is a characteristic of an organizational culture that fosters creativity. An organization in constant survival mode will have a difficult time with innovation because the energy is devoted to everything but creativity. There is no margin for error, so innovation is impossible. So, what type of culture encourages innovation?

- One that has a clear, aspirational vision that everyone believes in.
- One that encourages failure for the sake of exploring new ideas.
- One that has an intimate knowledge of its customers for the sake of developing products that meet their needs, not just data collectors to improve direct marketing effectiveness.

In many companies, especially those that put profits first, innovation is an inorganic strategy, usually acquired by investing in start-ups. Often these acquired people or organizations don't last because the ecosystem does not support their way of doing things. The pressures from the finance department to cut costs—and the pressure from senior leadership to deliver results—constrict the very characteristics and creativity that made them a successful target in the first place. Just remember, innovation is a cultural issue and nothing less. An honest assessment of how the environment encourages or discourages creativity and innovation is a necessary step if a company finds itself in dire need of customer connection.

REFLECTIVE EXERCISES

1. Does your organization have a clear aspirational vision that everyone believes in?

_____

_____

_____

_____

_____

2. As you consider the soul of your company–it's energetic vibe–does it reflect the energy necessary to deliver on the outcomes required as communicated by the CEO?

_____

_____

_____

_____

_____

3. Is there the requisite commitment and urgency to these outcomes or is that energy more centered around achieving comfortable objectives and modest aspiration?

_____

_____

_____

_____

_____

SUMMARY/KEY TAKEAWAYS

Having awareness of the soul of a company is a crucial step in understanding and diagnosing the effectiveness of the culture. Oftentimes in our professional lives, we are so focused on thinking and reasoning that we forget to feel. This chapter is about acknowledging that weak or misaligned cultures create negative feelings for team members and equally, healthy, high-performing cultures create positive, energetic feelings that unlock creativity. It's these feelings that reflect the soul of the company and provide vital clues as to how functional things are and how adept the organization will be in innovating market-defining solutions. As mentioned earlier, I am meeting more and more executive and senior managers, especially in the strategic planning function, that are becoming disenfranchised with the organization's (or CEO) willingness to acknowledge threats and consider new concepts to stay on top. In these cases, the vision is merely a slogan, and the various parts of the organization aren't aligned toward achieving a common purpose, albeit sometime subconsciously. Having an aspirational vision is one thing, but it's important to pulse-check the organization and determine if the vision serves to align everyone to the common cause. If so, trust me, you will feel that vibe and the outcome is magical!

6

WHAT IS DYSFUNCTIONAL CULTURE?

"Refuse to inherit dysfunction. Learn new ways of living
instead of repeating what you have lived through."
– Dr. Thema Bryant-Davis, Author,
Professor of Psychology, Pepperdine University

I was first brought into Barclays to fix a problem they knew
they had but didn't know how to fix. They knew they didn't
have a great culture, but they chalked it up to poor effort
or inadequate management by the previous teams. This
is the definition of a dysfunctional culture. It's a business
that's aware it has a problem, and that problem is that what
they say they value is different than what they practice. The
tendency for leaders is to quickly pursue solutions to solve
the problem, often doubling down on the value-destroying
actions that created the problem, thus leading to tactical actions that treat the symptoms rather than the root cause.
The focus is on changing behaviors without considering
what is motivating those behaviors.

On a personal level, we all tend to do this. We know deep
down there's an issue, but rather than get to the root cause

of the issue, we distract ourselves with another self-help book, a new course to take, a new toy to enjoy, or a million other things that we do to avoid confronting what's really going on. We know something's broken, yet we don't dare figure out what. Why? Because it usually takes more time and draws the focus on changing ourselves rather than the external forces we want to blame. Understanding the core of the issue is uncomfortable and takes patience, confidence, and perseverance to see things through. Most importantly, the motivation to change must be greater than the emotional imprint from the past. That requires hard work. It often means you must get your hands dirty. And it always means change.

Anything dysfunctional will fight change at all costs. A broken culture is no different. This is what I experienced when I first came into Barclays. The company brought me in to fix a problem that everyone knew existed but never took the time to fundamentally address. That was my job. I knew what to do but had to discover how to do it at scale and fast.

Early in my tenure, I walked out of my office one evening and asked who wanted to go out for a drink. Most of my colleagues were working at their stations, shoulder to shoulder—apparently, people in my job didn't just invite the entire group out. Out of the thirty or so people within earshot, only three people said yes. I didn't know it yet, but they didn't even report to me. Coincidentally (or maybe not so coincidentally), all three were on work visas in the human resources group from Australia—young, smart, and unafraid to speak their minds. As we sat chatting, they asked what I thought of the company and about my plans to address the things I thought needed attention. I confidently told them, "This is just what I do," and shared stories of how we created a common culture at Washington Mutual while integrating something like thirty-two acquisitions.

What they said next stunned me a bit and set me back on my heels. They said, "Well, Mike, if you haven't noticed, your team is not overjoyed that they brought you in at such a high level from America. While your success at Washington Mutual is amazing, you had an entire company behind you. Nobody is standing behind you here." After trying to explain my plans, I was finally smart enough to ask if they had any suggestions, and they said yes.

They drew me a transformation map used at their previous jobs in Australia, showing how they had helped transform the culture at Quantas Airlines as consultants. This is exactly what I needed to hear. This was a structured plan that would be the centerpiece of the transformation plan to re-design the culture. I was very impressed—and moved—by the three of them and asked them to join my staff immediately and help launch the same type of transformation at Barclays. I knew what needed to be done and that this roadmap and methodology would be central to the effort. They accepted, and we stayed late after work every evening creating a map for Barclays, complete with a plan and narrative to bring those 30,000 colleagues along on this journey to become a functional culture. (We'll walk through each step of this Transformation Map later in the book because it's the blueprint to turn around any business in crisis.)

Despite the excellent work by my new colleagues and other select, trusted team members, we failed to move the needle very far. Now, how can I have just said that this transformation map is the key tool to begin a complete cultural transformation for any company in crisis, then say that it didn't work? One may have the keys to the car, but there is much required to drive that car. In the case of cultural transformation, the map is a necessity; but if it's not accompanied by several other key components, it merely becomes relegated to another corporate campaign. "This, too, shall pass" was the feeling of most of the workforce. This map alone wasn't enough to make them see that we needed to authentically change, not just do the same things better. The transformation plan never fully succeeded to improve business results because the need to change wasn't accepted by the leadership team.

This was a few months before the *Whistleblower* program aired. The plan I proposed earlier wasn't all that different from the plan I proposed after the BBC pulled the rug out from under our feet. Don't get me wrong; we had begun to change the energy in the organization, and employee engagement scores began to climb, but it just didn't translate to business improvement. Why? Because absent an existential threat, change was more of a conceptual exercise and not broadly accepted as a necessity—especially not to the degree where we had to fundamentally rethink who we were. Unfortunately, just like in our personal lives, we sometimes need a threat to materialize before we accept that it's time to change. What I hadn't fully appreciated was that while the transformational map and the new direction in which we set out were important, they alone were not enough. In our monthly performance reviews before the board, questions about our lack of tangible progress were getting more and more pointed. I was only able to show green shoots of progress, promising that rising employee engagement would lead directly to productivity gains. And it would, only it was happening too slowly.

I still clearly recall when a senior leader walked by me in the hall, and I asked what his team was doing to catch up on their plan where they had fallen far, far behind. He gave me a huge smile, patted my shoulder, and said reassuringly, "Don't worry, Mike. The things you're changing are hugely helpful, and we're going to be fine. You'll see the business performance picking up very soon." My gosh, I wanted to believe this nice man! He was so confident and said the right things, but he was also terribly misguided. His performance would never recover, and, unfortunately, he didn't last long in his role either.

This is the challenge with change. Unless we believe in the vision of a better future and attach higher emotions to its fulfillment, change seems illogical. This great guy, leading an important group, didn't know what he didn't know. And I say that without placing judgment; after all, we all have situations where we're unconsciously incompetent. The challenge was to make the entire organization aware of this so that they became consciously incompetent. I know that looks like a misprint, but what I mean is that when they knew that they didn't know, they became students, and true learning could begin. Different leaders embraced this reality at different speeds and in different ways. Many of the people who reported to me directly would never make the shift to leading and inspiring in the high-performing organization we were going to build. Sadly, we needed a crisis to wake everyone up from the dream of complacency. I needed to show that there was a way to create a culture where we over-perform in every area. To do that, we had to see the world in a drastically different way.

It's important to revisit that another sign of a dysfunctional culture is team members who are inordinately focused on survival. All human beings will—depending on our per-sonality and values—express the survival mechanisms dif-ferently. In order to transform the ecosystem into a highly functional organization, we needed to be creative, which required an open, curious emotional state, thinking more broadly, and considering all possible options. When an or-ganization or an individual is in a perpetual state of survival, the opportunity to explore other solutions disappears. If a lion were rushing across a field toward you, your world shrinks into one or two possible options: running or freez-ing. This is not a situation where creativity flourishes. It's a time of fear, panic, and survival as your ability to ponder various solutions will be extremely limited.

The parallel is that if an organization is dependent on at-tracting and retaining high-performing individuals, there needs to be an energy inside the organization stronger than mere survival in order to thrive. Done right, this builds a sense of security. There is the understanding that if the person doesn't perform well, certain things need to happen, but if this becomes the primary focus, the survival instincts will kick in, creativity will be limited, and performance will ultimately suffer. To bring this philosophy to life, I wanted to remove barriers to high performance, aka negative stress points, while increasing urgency—the metabolic rate of the organization. I wanted to move from a culture of fear to a culture of creativity.

A dysfunctional culture may be closer to you than you may have ever imagined. Maybe this is why you chose this book. You just haven't been able to put your finger on it. You're not quite sure what is wrong, and maybe you're worried about figuring out what the real problem is because you're unsure what will happen once you open that box. You're right to be worried. Once you do open the box, you will face resistance. Resistance is inevitable. Later in the book, I'll show you how to overcome this and how to create a journey that everyone inside the organization can believe in.

But first, it's important to appreciate and truly understand the current state (the symptoms) and the causes. Once you find the dysfunction, you can begin to create the emotional alignment and motivation necessary to take the next steps. Almost every business faces this to some degree. Although each situation is unique, when they fall from grace, they fall the same way. I've had senior leaders tell me that things have never been better, and they're blessed with the most positive culture ever—only to see things completely fall apart later. Boeing, Wells Fargo, Enron, and Washington Mutual were at their all-time high in confidence and share price when crises struck. While it was fatal for Enron and Washington Mutual, and it did cost many senior leaders at Boeing and Wells Fargo their jobs—including both CEOs—it doesn't have to end this way.

There is a tendency to think that doing more of the same is good enough or that more training will suffice, rather than a complete rebuilding. Dysfunction is born through this disconnect. The problem is that many leaders look at the wrong symptoms, which leads them to diagnose the wrong problems. It's only logical that if the causes of underperformance are not understood, the solutions will be less effective.

If morale is low and turnover of high performers is high, more training is not the answer. If financial results are not adequate, intensifying managerial oversight and performance management alone is not the answer. You have to do an audit of the ecosystem to see the root causes of the underperformance. And I say this with extensive, personal knowledge of the pressure underperformance can bring. If the organization is falling short in any area, the pressure to turn it around is incredibly intense. This pressure drives seemingly logical—yet totally inadequate—solutions because for the manager to keep their job, it's vital to project urgency, strength, and certainty that they know how to fix it. They must show that they are fully prepared to create a plan and execute it. This reaction drives the proliferation of tactical solutions that are managing the output rather than the input. It's difficult to explain to the board that, despite their desire to see higher numbers and recovery, the solution is in changing the culture. It's a tough sell, but it's necessary to set the table properly. Unless boards and leadership can become more aware of these warning signs, they won't see the storm until it hits.

REFLECTIVE EXERCISES

1. Would you say that the culture in your organization is dysfunctional? Why or why not?

_____

_____

_____

_____

_____

_____

_____

_____

_____

_____

_____

2. What are the warning signs that you wish the board could see and act on now?

_____

_____

_____

_____

_____

_____

_____

_____

_____

3. What things should your organization do differently to improve performance and unleash the group's latent talent and creativity?

_____

_____

_____

_____

_____

_____

_____

_____

_____

_____

_____

_____

_____

_____

_____

_____

_____

SUMMARY/KEY TAKEAWAYS

Although a crisis can provide the necessary motivation to drive a fundamental review of the business and its ecosystem, there are definite warning signs when things are amiss. It's sometimes believed that achieving a functional, high-performing culture is a destination, but in reality it's an ongoing process that requires frequent assessments to watch for early warning signs of a shift away from the core values.

In our case, the crisis proved necessary to get everyone's attention to the fact that we had become dysfunctional, but ideally you can begin to lay the groundwork now for evaluating the many variables that act as foghorns that the organization may be drifting off course.

7

THE FALL FROM GRACE WATERFALL

"Performance more often than not comes down to a cultural challenge, rather than simply a technical one."
– Lara Hogan, Senior Engineering Manager of
Performance, Etsy

Just like I experienced, any company is one phone call away from a crisis, no matter what they may think of their current state. This is the reality for every single business on the planet. Nobody's immune. At any point in time, someone or something can come along and turn the world upside down. Sometimes this is unpredictable, but most of the time it is predictable. There are warning signs. Once you know what these are, they are clear to see.

The problem is that these warning signs are difficult to see before it's too late. Some may see the warning signs but are unable to gain the necessary buy-in from their bosses to trigger a deeper review of concerns. Cultural erosion happens very slowly, and those at the top have a very difficult time believing there is a reason for alarm. This is especially so when the metrics are all pointing the right way. Concerns expressed about something as intangible as cultural shifts are easily dismissed as the views of someone who doesn't fit in or understand the bigger picture.

On the other hand, there can also be a tendency to cry wolf whenever a strategic shift occurs because people believe they will be adversely affected, or perhaps they just resist change. I speak glowingly about the culture at Washington Mutual Bank when I was there, but not everybody felt the same way about the effect of our rapid growth equally. Many of the "old guard" felt disenfranchised with the shift in how the company was run the bigger we got. It was difficult to discern, especially when one is feeling things change, but the inevitable changes necessary to operate a bank our size weren't always about culture–they were sometimes just an adaptation of the operating model.

This is what makes continuously assessing and monitor-ing corporate culture so difficult yet so necessary. The fall from grace happens like a waterfall. Each warning sign listed below crashes into the next like a domino:

- Success: If it grows like a weed, it might just be a weed.
- Arrogance: Believing we're too big or too good to fail.
- Values Shift: What you say and what you do become very different.
- Disconnection: Serving one's silo and losing sight of the common purpose.
- Disengagement: The loss of a shared vision.

Let's go a bit deeper into each of these warning signs.

1: SUCCESS

Growth is at the heart of every successful business but difficult to sustain, especially after a period of rapid expansion. Pressure builds inside the organization to maintain the previous success and growth rates, which creates an imbalanced focus on the metrics that reflect the desired outcomes. In the case of Enron, its downfall was the reckless use of derivatives in the flawed belief that this was an appropriate way to transfer risks to the special-purpose entities it had acquired. In the case of Wells Fargo, it was the relentless pursuit of industry-leading cross-sell ratios, regardless of how they achieved them. In the case of Washington Mutual, it was the pursuit of higher-risk lending to increase loan margins. In each of these examples, the crisis followed times of great success and historically high stock prices.

The very thing that created the success turned out to be the downfall.

However, there are a lot of organizations that are flying high with no signs that they've reached their peak, so this alone is not enough of a warning sign. The thing to watch for here is not the metric or outcome but rather how that result is achieved. Is your company selling its soul to maintain growth rates or create the illusion of success? Is its primary focus on proving itself to external audiences, namely stock analysts, to drive greater investor support and share prices? If so, watch for these other signs that your crisis may be just around the corner.

2: ARROGANCE

Confidence is a good thing. In fact, it's a crucial element in any successful endeavor. However, if taken too far, confidence becomes arrogance. And arrogance can be blind. Have you ever heard of "too big to fail"? I had a boss once say, "The seeds of failure are often sown in times of success." Gosh, was he ever right. Overconfidence can cause leaders to think they've "arrived" or cracked the code to higher performance. Think of culture as the equivalent of an organization's health index. Just like the human body, health needs to be constantly monitored because it is constantly changing. Disbelieving or not seeking the right data is arrogant and a dangerous flaw in leaders that sets them up for a rude awakening. Wells Fargo executives noticed early signs of mis-selling but saw it as a behavioral issue rather than a cultural one. Washington Mutual brought in many executives from respected organizations who arrogantly believed they knew better based on their past success, and they ignored early signs that things were spiraling downward. In fact, they doubled down on the flawed strategies that would ultimately spell the company's doom. It's this influx of outside talent that can bring about the next warning sign.

3: VALUES SHIFT

Growth and success inevitably require a steady influx of talent—either from an acquisition or from recruiting externally to fill a role where a company needs more experience than internal candidates can provide. However, there can be a tendency to value new talent more highly than internal talent. While the company knows (and sometimes overstates) the flaws of internal candidates, it only sees the strengths of a new candidate. Praise of new talent may be warranted or may just be an example of the "new toy" syndrome.

With this influx of ideas, successes, and experience comes risks. A new team member brings with them strongly held beliefs about culture, and their subsequent values may or may not be consistent with the organization they are joining. Add to this an intense desire to put their thumbprint on the organization, and it may spell trouble. The executive that Washington Mutual recruited into the role of president once said, "I don't have a problem with your five core values of Human, Kind, Caring, Dynamic, and Driven, but I want to see more of the Driven." There are many problems with this statement, especially since our division had just experienced back-to-back years of 36 percent bottom-line growth. But the main issue is that this statement signaled a coming shift in values. By leaving the definition of Driven open to interpretation, it created an inconsistent understanding of this important value and how to apply it to the business.

When Boeing acquired McDonnell Douglas, the new corporation compromised between continuing with Boeing's traditional, time-honored value of highly engineered, safety-first planes and McDonnell Douglas' more rigorous focus on tight cost control and efficiency. This clash of values was never rationalized, and many speculate that it contributed to the Boeing 737 Max crisis. This is not to say that a company can't bring in people from the outside or change its culture to reflect a changing ownership structure or strategy. However, if values represent what the organization and leadership stand for and provide the framework for the type of culture an organization desires, it's crucial that the organization formally socializes any change in its stated values and aligns these changes with its purpose and vision. This effort provides context for the change and guidance to leaders on how to lead their teams. There can be no ambiguity, or the values and behaviors displayed will diverge from the stated values. This divergence creates the next stage of the waterfall from grace.

4: DISCONNECTION

If there are doubts about an organization's values, then there must be doubts about why the organization exists. What happens is that the stated purpose (which surely must include some benefit to customers who do business with an organization) becomes subordinate to the new de facto purpose. Focus inevitably shifts to financial performance, cost-cutting, or even financial engineering to hit profit targets. The behaviors required to focus primarily on financial results may be quite different than the behaviors required to support the original vision and purpose. The organization's leadership enters survival mode—with the rest of the company soon to follow—bending and even ignoring rules to achieve the results required to survive. This shift can be detrimental to the company, its customers, and its shareholders.

5: DISENGAGEMENT

Trust is a vital component of any relationship, and organizations are nothing if not a collection of relationships. When the company culture devolves into one where the singular focus on financial results influences all planning and execution strategies, the communication becomes distorted. The company's leadership does one thing and says another. When the CEO stands up in front of a group of managers and states that employees are their most valuable resource, then spends the rest of the time discussing cost saves, personnel cuts, and stricter performance management systems, it comes across as disingenuous.

Imagine preparing to hike across the desert, and the guide informs you that water is your most important resource, then promptly tells you to pour some of it out. In other words, while the messages of cost-cutting and staff reductions may be non-negotiable and necessary, it's crucial to communicate this in ways that are authentic and (for lack of a better phrase) adult-to-adult. No one is fooled when the hero statements about the values of the company are superseded by actions that say the true values are something different. This virtue signaling is much more apparent than many leaders believe and sows discord that results in disengagement. This is why employee engagement is such a powerful health indicator of the quality of corporate culture. It's by no means the only indicator, and there are challenges with over-reliance on this one metric, but there are more relevant ways to gather employee feedback.

Disengagement leads to the migration of talent, which is also a key indicator of an organization's overall health. People are only willing to say so much in an employee engagement survey, so it's important to watch those who vote with their feet. Once trust erodes, the best and brightest begin to look for greener pastures and return recruiter calls that would have otherwise gone unanswered. Watch where new recruits go, either within the organization or outside of it. The best will sense their disconnect with the culture and seek an employer whose values match their own. People are attracted to an authentic, aligned, and intentional culture that produces a much higher ROI than the best strategy alone. This is not something that you can "complete." Keeping your culture relevant is like standing on a ball. It's a balancing act, and one can never let their guard down.

A company with a powerful culture is not immune to problems, but they are better prepared to anticipate and respond to the problems they do have. Healthy, functional cultures will have an entire team of people ready to work together and do what's necessary in ways that are consistent with the values of the company. By doing so, a company can emerge from challenging times even stronger than before. With a powerful, functional culture, profits are a logical outcome of doing the right things for all constituent groups, not just shareholders. As we experienced at Barclays, the financial results were significantly greater when we stopped treating profits as the primary motive.

REFLECTIVE EXERCISES

1. Are there any blind spots by leadership in your organization that might prevent them from an honest assessment of the culture?

_____

_____

_____

_____

_____

_____

_____

_____

2. Can you sense any disconnect between the values the organization states are most important and which values are displayed every day?

_____

_____

_____

_____

_____

_____

_____

_____

3. Is there any evidence of virtue signaling in your organization? If so, how does the resulting disconnect between leadership, and the rank and file show up?

_____

_____

_____

_____

_____

_____

_____

_____

_____

_____

_____

SUMMARY/KEY TAKEAWAYS

Assessing the health of the culture within an organization can be challenging, especially in times of success. Knowing that a massive fall from grace awaits those who fail to recognize the signs should prove to be enough motivation to do a deeper dive into the connection between behaviors and values throughout every layer of the organization. Those inside the organization feel the culture every day, so understanding their perception of its connection to the values is crucial, especially beyond simplistic employee engagement surveys. For example, having a finger on the pulse of employee migration can be a very beneficial tool to provide insights into the perception of the ecosystem by employees, especially if talent migrates outside the organization. Leaders should spend as much time assessing the culture as they do measuring the P&L in order to avoid the potentially catastrophic outcomes that may be just one phone call away.

8

WHEN GIANTS FALL FROM GRACE

"Everyone pulls for David,
Nobody roots for Goliath."
– Wilt Chamberlain

Starbucks is a perfect example of a company that survived a self-imposed cultural crisis. After building a phenomenal brand over the '80s and '90s, Howard Schultz stepped aside, and Starbucks began to lose its focus by venturing into music and films and over-expanding dramatically. The culture shifted away from providing the "moments" that made Starbucks so popular. The stock price plummeted from a high of $18 in 2006 to $4.50 by 2008. This forced Howard Schultz to return and bring back the coffee culture and focus on customer experience. He famously closed every location for a day to retrain every barista, thus transforming the culture and bringing the share price up to an all-time high of $106. Did he incorporate a change in strategy? Absolutely. But his focus was on bringing back the values and customer-centric culture that made Starbucks famous in the first place.

Another example of a fall from grace is Wells Fargo. For a period of time, I held a business account with them. One day, I had an issue and called their customer service. They listened as I told them about my trouble with verifying a transaction, but they stopped me short by saying, "I can sort this for you, but it will be easier if we close this account and open a new one with more features, linked to a savings account." Why couldn't they just sort out my problem? The answer points to the reason Wells Fargo became one of 2016's greatest scandals.

For many years, Wells Fargo had the best retail banking model in the world. Their return on investment was the highest. Their return on equity was the highest. Their customer loyalty was the best in the industry. They had the greatest number of services per household, averaging between seven and eight where most banks only had three or four. From the outside, they had a great model led by a great team. They had the numbers to prove it and kept growing year after year. Yet all was not well on the inside, and it was these industry-leading numbers that proved to be their downfall.

Wells Fargo didn't build their success on the back of a great culture but rather a very successful cross-selling machine. They were great at getting their customers to sign up for multiple services by cross-selling saving accounts, credit accounts, mortgages, loans, insurance, and more. They realized it was the most effective way to grow their business. It underpinned their entire success; as time went by, they doubled down on these efforts and pushed their employees harder and harder. Increasingly aggressive sales targets became the theme of performance management discussions. Under this intense pressure to deliver, employees became very creative in the ways they survived. As early as 2011, customers started reporting that they had accounts for which they didn't sign up, plus some accounts that listed false addresses. Once this came to light, Wells Fargo leadership took the seemingly bold step to fire over 5,000 employees, reporting that they wouldn't tolerate this fraudulent behavior. Yet, they did nothing to change the underlying culture. The same intense management philosophies and tactics remained. The same incentives to cross-sell at all costs were still in place. They had simply replaced one set of people with a new set, believing the people were the problem.

In 2016, they were caught red-handed once again. More customers noticed on their credit reports that they had savings accounts and credit accounts they had never opened. Investigators later found millions of fraudulent accounts like these where Wells Fargo employees signed customers up for new services without their consent. Why did they do this? Nobody in the leadership structure directed these employees to do this, nor did they condone it, but through their intense drive to maintain industry-leading numbers and impress stock analysts, they had created an environment where survival was paramount, even if it meant compromising personal and corporate values. Ultimately, this culture crisis cost the company over $3 billion in fines and cost the CEO his job with personal fines of over $17 million. Incredibly, they still believed they could fix the problem internally, elevating their new CEO from within, which ultimately cost him his job when even more problems came to light. Today, their share price is roughly half of what it was in 2018. That tells you something about the ROI of a healthy culture.

Enron is an even more dramatic example of a giant falling. Practically overnight, Enron went from being one of the world's most powerful businesses to, well, nothing. Thousands of people lost their jobs—many of them had been totally unaware of what was going on. I imagine they were initially proud to work for Enron—a strong, powerful company with strong results that, in their minds, would no doubt continue to grow and prosper.

Enron's demise came about because its leadership team had fooled regulators with fake holdings and off-the-books accounting practices for years. They used special purpose vehicles and special purposes entities to hide their mountains of debt from investors and creditors. For instance, they would build a new power plant and immediately claim its projected profits on the books, even though it had yet to make a cent. If the revenue from the power plant was less than the projected amount, they would transfer the asset to an off-the-books corporation; instead of taking the loss, it would go unreported. This meant Enron could simply write off anything unprofitable without hurting the bottom line. They took risks but refused to accept any consequences that came with them. To people both inside and outside of the company, all looked well. Those at the top of Enron's hierarchy set this precedent. It filtered down as they built a ruthless culture full of people who only cared about the endgame. So, while it took almost two decades for Enron to climb its way to the top, it only took a few months to slip into the history books. Early in 2001, Enron was flying high with a share price of $90.75 per share, surging from $30 per share just a couple of years earlier. Stunningly, the share price plummeted to $0.26 per share within a year when they finally filed for bankruptcy. The price for a culture built on compromised values was $74 billion in lost shareholder value.

This is the impact a soured and dysfunctional culture can have, and the worst part is that while all these examples of cultural decline are quite visible and known to all, companies around the world continue to do the same things that compromise their reputations and even existence, inevitably causing more corporate crises and scandals.

REFLECTIVE EXERCISE

1. Does your organization exhibit any, or all, of the characteristics of the organizations that fell from grace?

_____

_____

_____

_____

2. Given the tremendous loss of reputation and shareholder value, why do you think organizations fail to course-correct prior to a fall from grace?

_____

_____

_____

_____

3. If culture is largely about how an organization practices its values when nobody is looking, what would an objective observer's reaction be if they could see how your organization operates behind the scenes?

_____

_____

_____

_____

4. If the public could see how your organization operates on a daily basis, what would be the reaction?

_____

_____

_____

_____

SUMMARY/KEY TAKEAWAYS

In the previous chapter, I shared the five characteristics of companies that have fallen hard, which are success, arrogance, shifting values, disconnection, and disengagement. Doing a deeper dive into each of the four examples shared in this chapter of giants falling from grace, you can see the commonality between all of them and the factors prevalent prior to their crash. Again, each of these companies was at an all-time high before the fall and it would have been nearly impossible to predict the dire consequences that awaited each. But my belief is that the employees inside the organizations had an inkling, at some level, that things were beginning to drift. Even if a catastrophe was not foreseen, they would have seen enough smoke to know there was a fire somewhere. So, the key takeaway here is that when considering the effectiveness of a culture, the leadership must look deeper than simply the financial performance or share price of the organization or even beyond the other key performance indicators that surely showed up green in each of the examples I've given. It's crucial to give the culture audit more than just a passing thought because it's necessary to monitor, measure, and measure often.

9

CULTURE AND BRAND

"In this ever-changing society, the most powerful
brands are built from the heart. Their foundations are
stronger because they are built with the strength of the
human spirit, not an ad campaign."
– Howard Schultz, CEO, Starbucks

It's necessary to repeat that culture is intrinsically linked to
brand. Culture is the company's brand expressed internally,
while brand is the company culture expressed externally.
Therefore, the key constituent for culture is employees, and
the key constituent for brand is customers. Obviously, there
are other constituents for an organization—such as capital
markets, regulators, and the broader community the organization supports—so the challenge for leadership is not to
balance the needs of each constituency group, as is often
quoted. Rather, it is to *meet* the needs of all the groups in
a balanced way. When leadership overemphasizes one constituency, culture diverts from that which the company says
they stand for into a state of imbalance. Again, this isn't
saying that there aren't logical reasons to focus on one pri-

mary constituency for a time, but it's crucial to monitor this divergence as it can signal a more permanent shift in core values that takes the company in unexpected or undesirable directions. This is when the company's culture separates from its brand, creating inauthentic and hypocritical messages, which leads to an accidental culture.

What happened at Barclays is a case in point. For several years, the primary focus had become about harvesting profits rather than investing in the future. The human aspect of the business, namely customers and employees, was lost in the equation. This then led to a leadership team whose energy was directed toward managing results rather than the process necessary to drive the results and fulfill the stated vision of being "The Best Bank in the UK." We needed to reset the ecosystem in a way that allowed everyone to flourish and perform at their very best. The BBC gave us the spark.

We now faced the challenge of using that spark to ignite a fire through the rest of the organization. Motivation alone doesn't produce this, and the reason comes down to human psychology.

Thanks to the *Whistleblower* program, I finally had the catalyst I needed to create change and reform the entire culture, but I knew it was just a start. We had to rally the troops and create a movement that gave them the desire to change. Not just those at the top of the hierarchy, but all 30,000 in the workforce. Not because the leadership team told them to, but because they wanted to. We had to create a journey for everyone—one they could believe in, be proud of, and that would once again shine a light on Barclays' vision.

REFLECTIVE EXERCISE

1. Does your organization have an area of focus that is taking away from investing in the future?

_____

_____

_____

_____

_____

_____

_____

_____

_____

2. Does your leadership spend as much time on defining, monitoring and measuring the culture as they do on brand awareness?

_____

_____

_____

_____

_____

_____

_____

_____

3. What decisions needs to be made to keep the focus on the vision of being "the best" instead of only focusing on short-term results?

_____

_____

_____

_____

_____

_____

_____

_____

_____

_____

_____

_____

SUMMARY/KEY TAKEAWAYS

If where you focus determines where you spend your energy—and it does—the same is true for an organization. It's typical for companies to consider the impact to the brand on nearly every decision that is made. This is because the more powerful the brand perception of an organization, the more pricing flexibility they have. For example, this is why prices for bags, purses, and cosmetics vary dramatically, based almost solely on the power of the brand. Absent that branding power, products risk becoming commoditized. The same principles hold true for culture. If an organization has a weak or poorly defined culture, they are forced to pay above market wages in order to fill key roles, but even that is not guaranteed to retain talent that will take the next higher-paying job. So besides understanding the risks of a toxic or dysfunctional culture, it's important for organizations to consider the upside of a powerful, functional culture. There needs to be an awareness that the significant improvement in business performance warrants intense focus on optimizing the organization's culture.

10

THE RELEVANCE OF MANAGEMENT

"Ultimately, it's on the company leaders to set the tone.
Not only the CEO, but the leaders across the company."
– Tim Cook, CEO, Apple

This journey, as it always does, began with leadership. We had to rethink the type of leadership that best fit the new direction and clearly define *leadership relevance*. We had an underperforming organization in crisis. To reset the culture, we needed to jar the management team by asking this most basic (and shocking) question: "Given the state of the business and your responsibility to deliver results, can you tell me how you define managerial relevance?" I asked this question in a meeting of about fifteen senior managers. It was clear they had never thought about their ownership of the company's state. In their minds, we needed them to become more directive, strengthen their grip on performance, and hold their employees accountable for failing to hit their targets.

In other words, the senior managers were fine; we just needed everyone below them to change. This is a prescrip-

tion for disappointment. We needed every single person—
most obviously the senior leaders—to examine their role in
the dysfunctional culture, take ownership in first changing
themselves, and only then ask their charges to change. To
say it more succinctly, *the leadership team believed we were
solving the underperformance problem when the problem we
needed to solve was the working environment that caused the
underperformance.*

We needed leaders who effectively conveyed and magnified
the vision, not just tactical drivers of the business results.
As we set out to create our new and intentional culture, it
was clear that nothing would change if we couldn't redefine what our leaders stood for and how they could help us
become the best bank in the world.

To move away from the type of management that led to an
under-performing culture, we had to give managers a new
vision of their role. In this new model, they were to unlock
discretionary energy, not merely demand results. Shortly
after I arrived, I met with a new district director who proudly proclaimed that he had just recently transferred into that
role and had already replaced more than 70 percent of his
direct reports. He said this with pride, intending to convey
that he was a courageous, dependable guy. He didn't say it
with malice; clearly, he was following his marching orders.
Instead of focusing on the things I would have expected a
manager-of-managers to bring to my attention, his focus
was on changing the behaviors of his charges and convinc-
ing me that I could count on him to do the tough things—
to be a top player, driving new expectations and demanding
more from his people.

Instead of passing judgment, I needed to model a more mature view of his role and increase his understanding of running a business. If I wanted him to create an environment that produced success, not fear, I needed to model that myself. I led him into a conversation about his view of the BBC program and what he thought were the core drivers in the organization that needed attention. The change in his demeanor was palpable. He saw that he could speak openly—without fear of retribution—and he began to trust that I was not interested in window dressing or papering over the fundamental challenges his team faced each day. I told him that we owed it to our colleagues to show that we cared about helping them succeed by providing the necessary support. He then told me the things he thought needed to be considered, such as incentive systems, broken processes, and out-of-date technology. This was priceless information for developing a transformation strategy.

It all starts with listening. If an employee has all the right tools and support and still can't seem to succeed, then we will do the right thing for the organization by making the necessary changes—whether that means transferring them to a more suitable role or "decruiting" them by terminating their employment. Strength and compassion need to go hand in hand. When a person is unhappy or a poor fit in the culture, their colleagues know it. They carefully watch how the leader handles these situations because this determines their judgment on the worthiness of the leader. A leader who rails on about needing to boost performance but tolerates habitual underperformers is seen as weak. If we expect people to serve the brand and support the culture, it's imperative that everyone—managers included—is held accountable through actions.

This points to one of the biggest challenges in leading a transformation. One cannot delegate a cultural overhaul to a project manager, or it becomes relegated to a short-lived campaign. All too often, leaders launch a cultural transformation by assigning the job to a trusted senior aide and then attempt to monitor progress from afar. This does not work because this approach signals that the reform program is just a tactical campaign in response to a problem, not a strategic overhaul of how the company does business. Nothing says "This, too, shall pass" faster than a leader who states that this culture change is their highest priority but is visibly disconnected from its development. Campaigns have a very short life cycle. They all start with passionate speeches, acronyms, charts, and reminders. But the flurry of activities begins to fade as focus inevitably shifts to the problems of the day. If a leader wants to transform the culture, then their philosophies, vision, and voice must reflect the holistic changes that need to occur.

While on the board of Santander, I was asked by the CEO—one of the most dynamic leaders I have ever met—to review her cultural transformation program and provide input on how to make it succeed. She had assigned the primary role to a very smart woman in a senior role who had done a great job pulling the program together. However, my observation was that not all executives supported it, much less promoted it, because they did not see it as coming from the CEO, nor did they even believe the culture could be transformed in anything less than ten years—which were the exact words of the HR director. The head of the business knew his numbers inside and out and had a deep understanding of all the competitors but had very little interest in understanding the current state of their culture, much less buying into the CEO's desired future state. So even though all the right pieces were in place, the program fizzled out and had little impact beyond the excitement of the launch phase. The impetus of the transformation must come from the top, and all leaders need to be held accountable for leading their team through the transformation, with no exceptions.

When I launched the transformation program at Barclays, not everyone agreed on what we should do or how to do it, but they all agreed we needed to do something. The more I listened to the feedback from the various executives, the more convinced I became of the direction we needed to take. I was prepared to encourage those leaders who couldn't—or wouldn't—adapt to explore careers elsewhere. In one small group meeting, a fast-track, top-talent manager asked if I was willing to watch her leave the company if she disagreed with the new direction. She asked what I would do if more executives joined her and left. My response was immediate and direct. I believed in my heart of hearts that what we were doing was going to be successful. If I compromised on my core beliefs, the transformation would be short-lived. Plus, my philosophies are deeply rooted in the belief that managerial courage is funded by the ability to recruit—internally or externally.

My response was that we would seek to have the very best person in the world at every position. And if someone did not buy into who we were going to become, then they could not be the best person in the world for that job. My only question for her was, "Are you the best person in the world at your job?" Everyone in the room was stunned. They knew right then that this transformation was not the usual "This, too, shall pass" campaign. They knew that it was bigger than any one person and that I was 100 percent committed to this direction. To this senior leader's credit, she genuinely did not think the new direction would work for her, so shortly after this meeting, she left the organization to join a competitor where she was very successful. Today, she is the CEO of a large organization in a different industry and is doing a fabulous job. She stayed true to her heart and I to mine. She thrived after leaving Barclays, and we thrived after she departed because her role was assumed by her talented colleague who was more suited to the direction we were going to take the organization. The outcome was perfect for all.

As things evolved, many executives left and were replaced by top senior leaders who bought into the vision and thrived once given the chance to perform on a larger role. In turn, their managers embraced the changes, adapted, and performed incredibly well. This is not just a testament to the changes but also to the fact that they were the architects of the new culture. They openly shared what needed to be addressed for them to do a good job, fulfill the vision, and receive the appropriate reward. For this majority, I was pushing on an open door. I just had to get them to believe that putting the right people in the right jobs, providing the resources necessary to succeed, and showing a deep appreciation for success would bring about a step-change in performance. And it did. We redefined what we thought was possible in every dimension of performance and discovered the joy of working in alignment with values and purpose.

REFLECTIVE EXERCISE

1. Have you seen any examples in your organization where issues are labeled behavioral when, in fact, they're cultural?

_____

_____

_____

_____

_____

_____

_____

_____

_____

2. Is your most senior leadership aligned, or do you see times when they pursue separate agendas?

_____

_____

_____

_____

_____

_____

_____

_____

_____

3. If your culture needs to be refreshed or even overhauled, who do you think should be charged with overseeing this?

_____

_____

_____

_____

_____

_____

_____

SUMMARY/KEY TAKEAWAYS

Often, when leaders don't like an outcome or there is a shortfall in performance, they're quick to demand new or better training programs. But at times, the issues are merely reflecting inadequacies of the leadership and the ecosystem they are responsible for overseeing. The root of the analysis about which solution is most appropriate begins with the understanding that people are reasonable. This literally means that, unless they are not clinically sane, they are *able* to *reason*. So, when groups of individuals disappoint, it most often means that they are behaving in a certain way because they reasoned it to be either correct or the best way for them to keep their jobs. Of course, this is not always the case, but in my experience, more often than not, the key contributing factor to issues of underperformance are caused by leadership that is lacking in some way.

By the same logic, the leadership is also acting reasonably, at least in their mind; therefore, once these issues are known and brought to the fore, it's absolutely crucial that any fundamental review and subsequent relaunch of the culture come from the top. And the conviction by this leader about the direction of travel must be so firm that they are willing to make the necessary changes to their team to reinforce the key messages and ensure delivery of the intended transformation. To be direct, this leader of leaders cannot delegate this responsibility, or they risk being part of the problem.

11

THE CHANGING ROLE OF LEADERSHIP

"Our best weapon for building the best culture is open and
honest feedback."
– Gina Lau, Team Operations, HelloSign

As unnatural as it may feel for a manager at any level to
ask themselves how they are relevant—especially with the
pressure to perform and produce results in ever-tightening
timeframes—the next step is equally, if not more, challenging: *rethink control.*

Many leaders today define their primary role as a control
function. In other words, their ability to exercise control
over their responsibilities determines their impact. Many
conversations about a manager's performance center around
complete knowledge of business data and the predictability of their team's performance, rather than on employee
engagement, growing their capability, and succession planning. Is it any wonder that the gap between workers and
management is growing? The wider this gap becomes, the
lower the employee engagement and their commitment to

the larger vision. There is no longer a shared purpose. Not only does this problem deteriorate performance, but it can sow the seeds of much larger problems.

The fact of the matter is that management is no longer a control function because management no longer controls the dissemination of all information. Employees can now access information online from various sources, meaning they are not at a disadvantage to their managers. If managers only rely on the information that the company shares with them, they may find themselves at a disadvantage to their employees who take the time to do the research.

What role does a manager play in today's workplace? For many generations, there was no way to access information other than what the corporate heads shared, so the leader's voice was vital to set direction and provide context for the work. Corporate structures began to imitate military leadership structures. Even as we evolved as a society, a select few always held the most important information. The risk is that those at the top can become completely disconnected from those on the front line. This outlook on leadership is dated and has been for quite some time now, but it's especially so today when anyone can access almost any information with the swipe of a finger.

The embedded flaw in the old model is that the separation of leadership and their support staffs from the employee base means that communications and policies from managers, internal communications departments, public relations, compliance, and legal can become so focused on protecting the company from potential risk that the messages become opaque, filled with empty jargon, and therefore, meaningless. It's almost as if the company forgets that their employees are functional adults, able to manage their lives away from work where they have no managerial oversight or guidance. They raise, educate, and care for their children. They honor familial and community cultures as important parts of their personal lives. They care for aging parents and survive personal crises. And they do all that without guidance or direction from their executives and company policymakers. Imagine that! It's almost as if managers believe that while their employees may be able to conduct their personal lives on their own, they are somehow different at work, totally dependent on the company leadership to provide vital policies and direction.

To attack this mindset during the transformation at Barclays, we coined the phrase "Adult-to-Adult Communication." Rather than treat our colleagues like they were incapable of grasping the finer art of performing their duties and serving their customers, we decided to speak openly and transparently and provide context for every challenge and decision.

Given this change in how we viewed the fundamental role of leadership, I knew that the only way we would succeed in our journey was to change the management model from "micro-managing" or "command and control" to "inspiring leadership." And we would do this by emphasizing leadership vs. management.

REFLECTIVE EXERCISE

1. How do at least three leaders at your organization define their relevance? How does this align with their personalities?

_____

_____

_____

_____

_____

2. Does your organization value communications that are transparent and provide necessary context? Or are they written primarily to protect the organization from legal and PR risks?

_____

_____

_____

_____

_____

3. What needs to be done to evolve "command and control" methods of operations to "inspiring leadership" strategies?

_____

_____

_____

_____

_____

SUMMARY/KEY TAKEAWAYS

Defining the role of leadership, especially in today's new reality caused by the pandemic, is essential to being able to ensure that each leader is relevant to their charges and to the company. In this chapter, I propose the notion that if a leader defines their primary role as performance driver or controller, they are not only behind the times, but they are limiting their ability to impact that which they are focused on managing. This challenge is even more pronounced when executive leadership values managers who obsess over their numbers and can recite them from memory at a moment's notice. Of course, an executive should feel confident that their managers have a handle on the business and are able to articulate their performance on key performance indicators, but knowing their people makes them so much more relevant to the company, the executive, and their employees. A key solution to creating a greater, more impactful, and relevant connection between a leader and their employees is to begin speaking adult to adult. The organization can still be protected from legal exposure, but the employees will perform better having a much fuller context to what's changing and, crucially, why it's changing.

12

LEADERS VS. MANAGERS

"Management is doing things right;
leadership is doing the right things."
– Peter Drucker

The shift from micro-managing to inspirational leadership
was an important journey within the journey, starting with
creating the case for change. Early in my career, I saw a pre-
sentation comparing a manager with a leader. These com-
parisons are common, showing a manager versus a leader:

Manager	Leader
Oversees process well	Charts the course
Strives to achieve balance	Shares a vision
Thinks in terms of execution	Motivates and inspires
Is comfortable with control	Focuses on empowering people
Sees problems as problems that need to be solved	Has a long-term strategic orientation

One of the things that struck me about this comparison was that the leader can tap into discretionary energy. This is the power of *want to* versus *have to* and is the difference between barely hitting the target and beating the stretch plan. To unleash this energy from a diverse group of people, a leader needs a high degree of emotional intelligence (EI) and empathy. If a leader takes the time to understand where their direct reports are coming from, what motivates them, and how best to support them, it is much easier to communicate direction, coaching, performance improvement ideas, and policy changes in relevant ways to the employee. This, in turn, creates a relevant leader.

This isn't easy to achieve, but there is a single word that keeps you on the right track: *Connection.* Connection requires empathy. A leader must connect and relate to people with empathy and mutual understanding, rather than merely providing direction. The objective is to guide employees toward a common vision within a specific framework.

The most effective leaders understand that every employee has their own goals and objectives for their career that they want to achieve, so they don't just communicate what the organization wants and needs from them. They also learn what that employee wants and needs from the organization. Knowing this and working with employees toward their mutual goals helps the leader more effectively motivate their employees and inspire higher performance.

This is connected leadership. It's simple in premise but complex in reality. It's even more challenging if one is in the middle of a crisis and needs to act quickly and decisively. During the COVID-19 pandemic, every company is in a crisis, no matter how well they handled the challenges of remote work.

For example, business leaders laud their efforts to respond to the "new normal" created by the pandemic and tell the outside world that their people have adapted and are thriving. However, Microsoft recently took a poll of over 30,000 workers that showed more than 40 percent are exhausted and considering leaving their jobs, and 56 percent say they feel overworked. Incidentally, only the most senior leadership group claimed that the organization is thriving. With many opportunities available to tech workers outside Microsoft, this presents a massive risk. If a company sets a mid-single-digit target percentage of regretted turnover (the loss of A players), having even a fraction of your workforce considering outside opportunities is potentially disastrous. I can't think of a more poignant example of disconnected leadership.

Improving corporate culture is not a new idea. Despite over twenty years of conversations about improving leadership practices and creating the "right" corporate culture, nothing has significantly changed. A Gallup poll shows that the percentage of employees who feel engaged in their work slipped from 33 percent in 2000 to 31 percent in 2019. This lack of engagement has huge costs to the organization—not to mention the well-being of its workers—and deeply challenges the fulfillment of the desired culture. Often, we underestimate the true cost of turnover, which includes the cost of hiring, onboarding, training, and severance. Then, add in the loss of productivity from an uninspired worker, including the productivity gap between when they leave and when their replacement is hired, as well as the lower productivity during the ramp-up time for the new employee. Finally, it's difficult to measure impact on other workers as they must pick up the slack when valuable team members move on, further damaging their morale. This is why estimates of the true cost of turnover show a range of 1.5-2 times the departing employee's salary.

Relevant leaders connect with their team and consider their needs. Besides just analyzing the cost of having a disconnected leader and a disengaged team, it's as important to understand the benefits and value of improved performance from truly engaged workers. This is often overlooked, but my experience at Barclays opened my eyes to the tremendous value of breakthrough performance driven by these truly engaged and inspired workers.

We improved productivity and efficiency simultaneously, meaning that we made twice the revenue on lower costs and did so while improving the customer experience, decreasing risk and, ultimately, customer advocacy. And it would not have been possible without resetting the relevance of our leaders and supporting them in transitioning to—and believing in—a new, connected way to lead.

We knew that we needed to change the definition of leadership. The next challenge was how to change it. The rest of this section will explore how we helped thousands of managers fundamentally change how they defined their roles.

REFLECTIVE EXERCISE

1. How would you define the difference between manager and leader? How many of the leadership boxes do you, or your boss, tick?

_____

_____

_____

_____

_____

_____

_____

_____

_____

_____

_____

2. What new techniques can you adapt to better "connect and relate" with your team? What suggestions would you give your boss?

_____

_____

_____

_____

_____

_____

_____

3. What employee needs is your organization not addressing?

_____

_____

_____

_____

_____

_____

_____

_____

_____

_____

SUMMARY/KEY TAKEAWAYS

Leadership relevance is not something that is typically dis-cussed, or even thought about for that matter. A leader would know the answer off the top of their head because they have already considered how best to lead their team, rather than merely relying on their title for proof of author-ity. Creating a connection with their organization or team is one of the most powerful ways to underscore a leader's relevance and create a highly functioning eco-system. But I am shocked that the issue of disconnected leadership is still so prevalent. Even accounting for the challenges presented by remote working, it's clear that managers are not able to connect with their staffs with shocking frequency. The con-clusion I have reached is that the wrong people are being promoted. Success at one level of the career ladder doesn't ensure success at the next level because often the skills to suc-ceed are quite different. And if a person is the right person, the organization is failing to prepare them for the new level, leaving them to learn on the job, which unfortunately can mean many unnecessary bumps along the way. To put it succinctly, the best way to win is with more prepared leaders and fewer entitled managers.

13

ACCOUNTABILITY THROUGH EMPOWERMENT

"It is not only what we do, but also what we do not do,
for which we are accountable."
– Molière, French Poet and Author

Those rooted in the old command and control leadership model—*which is a surprisingly large percentage of people*—will hear the above and nod in agreement as the concepts are certainly very universal. Maybe they're even willing to give up certain power and control, yet there will always be the caveat, *"But, how do I know that my team will deliver?"*

What I've described above takes a leap of faith. We know that "command and control" delivers limited results, but at a big cost in engagement. We must ask the questions: Does a "kinder, gentler" approach really work? And how does an empathetic manager handle those who underperform? Isn't this just a manager trying to be liked? The answer to these questions is crucial: The role of a leader is still to lead and hold people accountable to certain standards. Otherwise, it creates a flawed system. Each person on this journey must be held accountable for their work. It's a mistaken belief if one thinks that having empathy means that there is no accountability.

I've seen a lot of resistance over the years because people presume this approach is too soft and that it's giving people an opportunity to get complacent. Far from it. I believe that this approach does just the opposite. By treating employees as adults and sharing the vital context for the direction, each person knows exactly what their needed contribution is. If they come up short, they know that, too, because we measure everything and report frequently. I've always set high standards—much higher than merely hitting the plan—for myself and those around me, and I do everything in my power to keep each person accountable in their role and for the grander goals we're all striving toward. If they cannot (or will not) keep pace, they do not last long. It's as simple as that.

So many organizations want to give employees responsibility for an outcome, believing that this creates accountability. For true accountability to exist, the person with the responsibility must be given the authority necessary to make the decisions that lead to success—or failure—thus creating true accountability.

A healthy, high-performing culture of accountability can easily fall prey to a dangerous trend: moving decision-making further and further away from the customer. Highly educated technocrats and specialists are more frequently responsible for making decisions, but they are too distant from the business, the customer, and the many nuances involved in delivering the products and services to the customer. These decisions range from collecting and analyzing customer usage data to governing inventory levels and timing, as well as planning schedules for customer-facing outlets, product development, and promotion. While it makes sense to utilize the specialists and their skills to provide vital functions to the business, problems can arise when these departments are given the responsibility and authority to oversee their particular function, but the front line is accountable for the outcome of the programs or campaign. Here are some actual examples of the challenges this creates:

- Local store managers for a national retailer of home furnishings aren't allocated enough staff hours to cover a sale because the product team and the finance team didn't communicate with each other during a sales campaign. While the local store manager, with thirty-two years of experience, identified the conflict early on and predicted the outcome, she has no authority to override the staffing model. This leads to a crowded store, underserved and dissatisfied customers, and stressed staff members. Calls to the regional offices for any exceptions are required, but their availability is spotty on weekends—if they can be reached. Those regional offices must go to their finance counterparts to make exceptional staffing decisions. This leaves the store manager and staff feeling the pain, without any authority to make

common sense staffing decisions. Not only that but
the store manager's bonus is based on sales volumes
and customer satisfaction. A weekend of chaos and
unhappy customers could mean a reduction in her
bonus, as well as lost revenue for ancillary or add-
on sales of complementary items.

- A national hardware chain uses centralized
  inventory control departments—which use
  generalized information to model and dictate
  how much of each product is allocated to stores.
  They don't account for regional differences, local
  customs, or even local celebrations, leaving both
  customers and staff frustrated by the product
  selection, product shortages, and dead inventory
  of items that don't move. Store staff, who have
  no say in what products to order, are relegated to
  the role of apologists as they are helpless to assist
  a customer when, for example, there are several
  portable heaters but no air conditioning units on
  the shelves in July. Their centralized department
  advises them to blame COVID-19 disruptions in
  the supply chain, even while other products are
  adequately sourced.

- There is a public relations incident for a local
  grocer that requires a company response and is
  handled by the communications or PR department.
  These departments must follow rigorous processes
  to identify and minimize a plethora of risks.
  Guided by input from compliance and legal teams,
  these processes produce generalized, sanitized, and

useless responses that say nothing and are released
hours after customers have contacted the store
staff for information, leaving the local manager
to essentially create their own responses out of
necessity.

These challenges could be properly minimized if the people
or departments with the authority to oversee a function
were held accountable for the result or had a tighter connection with the customer-facing teams. Unfortunately, the
frontline staff often must produce answers that they do not
have while customer numbers, sales, and service scores drop.
The people who are responsible for making decisions about
the customer should also be the ones who bear the pain of
dissatisfied customers due to their decisions.

One solution is to give the frontline more capability to in-
tervene through better training and some authority to override policy in certain situations—based on an analysis of the
tradeoffs posed by such situations. This necessitates hiring
qualified managers and staff, providing the necessary training and reporting infrastructure, and subsequently holding
them accountable by assessing their performance in line
with risk management policies.

This solution creates the mindset that each store, branch, or
call agent is an important extension of the brand, not just a
cost center or necessary evil. The company's true costs would
go up, but the revenue per customer should increase at a
much higher rate. We witnessed this at Washington Mutual,
but it became even clearer at Barclays that we needed to give

those who worked directly with our customers the appropriate authority to make the best decision possible.

It's one thing to trust an experienced branch manager, but it's another to pass that trust on to tellers and those on the phones. There was a lot of understandable resistance to this idea. But we changed the focus from micromanaging the front-line teams to supporting them in making the best decisions, equipped with the proper information. Aligning responsibility, authority, and accountability changed the mindset of the workforce, which unleashed a new level of success and helped us unearth hidden gems deep inside our organization who became more engaged in their jobs than they ever thought possible.

Giving the front-line teams more authority to step up and succeed or fail created true accountability. Once you give someone the authority and freedom to do their job and provide the necessary guidance and goals, the responsibility for their success or failure rests in their hands. This approach to accountability is more demanding but results in significantly higher performance than the alternative.

REFLECTIVE EXERCISE

1. Which people within your organization have the decision-making authority when it comes to serving customers' needs? At what level of the corporate structure do these decision makers reside?

_____

_____

_____

_____

_____

_____

_____

_____

_____

2. How many levels removed from the customer are these decision makers? Who is ultimately held accountable then for their decisions?

_____

_____

_____

_____

_____

_____

_____

_____

3. What accountability and authority changes need to be made to improve customer experience while reducing employee stress?

_____

_____

_____

_____

_____

_____

_____

_____

_____

SUMMARY/KEY TAKEAWAYS

Accountability is a key pillar of any management philosophy. However, in order to hold someone accountable, they must have the necessary responsibility and authority to do the job. If authority and responsibility are not part of a person's makeup, true accountability is impossible. While it's more important than ever to gather and mine data, which is necessarily a central function's responsibility, and control costs, typically in the customer-facing roles, the effect has been to remove any local decision-making authority by the front lines. This disempowerment means that customers experience irrelevant service personnel more and more frequently, leaving them frustrated to get the answers needed or to solve their problems without having to escalate to a nameless person in a centralized role. This means an organization's customers are relegated to being in contact only with employees who have no control over the customer's experience. The effect is that customer loyalty suffers as the customer is less likely to expand their relationship with the company or even cease doing business with it altogether. This renders management speeches about the need to improve performance and hit targets meaningless and perhaps even hypocritical. Align these three components of responsibility, authority, and accountability, with an enlightened leader, and watch the business thrive like never before.

14

BUILDING TRUST

"Trust starts with trustworthy leadership. It must be built
into the corporate culture."
– Barbara Brooks Kimmel, Founder, CEO,
Trust Across America-Trust Around the World

Just as in any relationship, one of the very necessary components to creating and sustaining a high-performing culture, based on empowering employees is *trust*. You must show those you lead that you trust them to do their job. You're clear about the consequences if they break this trust, become complacent, or fail, but you show them that you trust them enough to do their job. And employees, in turn, must trust their managers. Mutual trust creates a sense of security, which is a vital component of employee engagement.

I know many managers who pride themselves on creating discomfort because they believe this discomfort creates workers who are forced to try harder than they would otherwise. This approach relates to that manager's view of human nature, as the operative belief is that humans are basically lazy and need to be driven, micro-managed and pushed to get the best out of them. This becomes a self-fulfilling prophecy, as a worker with initiative, independence, creativity, and highly self-motivated (aka top performer) would not tolerate working for a boss like that and will leave to pursue their career elsewhere. Meanwhile, the opposite type of person who either likes knowing exactly what's expected and appreciates the direction or perhaps doesn't feel like they have any other job alternatives remains. But as much as I don't support micro-managing, it's clear that both approaches require mutual trust for the relationship to be a successful one.

One of the striking things I've noticed in discussing this topic with others is that some managers, particularly in engineering or programming in the tech field, not only fail to build trust, but can actually appear to be disinterested in even connecting with workers enough to show that they care to build a trusting relationship. One group of recent EMBA graduates recently told me that even while working in person is permitted a few days each week, some of them rarely spoke with their boss, either virtually or in person. One man told me that only when he quit did his boss contact him to see what could be done to save him from leaving. This was the first time his boss had actually indicated any interest in the employee, as the only other times they had spoken were when the boss asked about the status of a project. I can't say for certain, but I wouldn't be surprised if this boss chalked up the employee departure to the disloyalty of "this new generation." I would counter that if this is a generational issue, it's because that industry is creating a new type of manager—a talented individual contributor who is wholly unequipped or unprepared to manage people, much less be seen as a leader. People don't quit companies; they usually quit bosses, and the responsibility to build a functional relationship based on trust is that of the manager's. This is so basic that it's hard to believe we're even talking about it, but you would be shocked if I told you the name of this Fortune 100 company.

Trust is crucial, even in the case of an underperformer. Not only between that employee and their manager, but with the other team members, as well. When a manager tolerates underperformance, others take notice and their trust in that manager is eroded. Trust is possible when everyone on the team is serving the purpose of the organization, not an individual. When a manager allows underperformance, they are letting the team down, so it's imperative that the employee is given all the tools and knowledge to succeed but is held accountable if they still don't meet expectations. The rest of the team is watching so how the manager handles these situations determines their level of trust and respect.

Often, if the manager has done a good job of overseeing the performance improvement plan, the employee will self-select and transition to different roles that are more suitable to their talents within the organization, or they will pursue their career outside the company. However, in a trusting work environment, employee engagement surges and the vast majority of people will thrive and prove their value in surprising and rewarding ways—for themselves and the organization—by over-performing and exceeding stretch goals. They are engaged in serving the purpose of the organization and are inspired to play their role in the mission. This inspiration comes from a place within. It comes back to an *"I want to do this"* attitude instead of *"I feel like I have to."*

This creates an entire workforce that wants to turn up to work each day and appreciates the importance of their role. As a leader, you have more time and energy to lead instead of looking over shoulders, checking boxes, and micromanaging your entire team. Your contribution is so much greater than simply reviewing the numbers and catching people out if they can't explain every detail by memory.

Even with all the data showing the power of employee engagement, "know your numbers" is still a prevalent management style by managers who are trained that their highest and best use is to manage the results. Of course, the leader must deliver results, but the teams I've served have proven time and time again that the most effective way to overdeliver is to stop managing numbers and instead manage the process, starting with understanding and connecting with your people. This creates mutual accountability and a strong connection that is only possible in a trusting relationship.

REFLECTIVE EXERCISE

1. How would you rate the level of trust in your organization? What are the drivers that you considered when making this rating?

_____

_____

_____

2. What does the company do to promote trust? What does it do that erodes trust?

_____

_____

_____

_____

3. What changes need to be made within your organization so that your key leaders stop managing numbers and start managing the process?

_____

_____

_____

_____

SUMMARY/KEY TAKEAWAYS

Trust is a vital component in any relationship, work relationships included. Trust is created in various ways, including acting in ways that are consistent with the policies and values of the company, communications that are clear and aligned with the purpose of the organization, and behaviors that reinforce everything the organization stands for. The primary goal of leadership is to create this trusting relationship so that even in the most difficult situations, the organization can rely on them to act in ways that serve the team, not just an individual.

Empowerment is a key driver of high performance, and the root of empowerment is trust. Even in the most challenging of situations, where an employee is underperforming, developing a high level of trust empowers the manager to meet expectations and do the right thing, which is often the hard thing, to ensure a good outcome for the individual and the team.

15

THE MINDSET OF GREAT LEADERSHIP

"Leadership is a mindset in which one is unapologetically
driven towards their goals and in behaving accordingly,
inspires those around them to join in."
– Steve Maraboli, Behavioral Scientist, Bestselling Author

There's a phrase I like that says, *"A players hire A players,
whereas B players hire C players."* This sums up the difference
between the old outlook of leadership and the new one, un-
derscoring the mindset of today's most successful leaders.
Naturally, this depends on the size of the company, but the
leader shouldn't want or need to be the smartest person in
the room. The role of a leader isn't to be the best but rather
to hire and manage the best. Where outdated managers
bring in people they are comfortable managing and controlling, a strong leader focuses on hiring people who can make
the organization stronger from day one until one day they
are qualified to take over their job. This is the mindset of a
secure person and a great leader.

One day when I still worked at Washington Mutual, I received a call from a regional manager with the responsibility

to oversee more than twenty branches. He had joined us through an acquisition of a company that was very much a command-and-control culture. "Mike," he said, "we have to hire a new assistant branch manager in Palm Springs, so I wonder if you could come out and do the interviews with me next week."

"Sure!" I said. "I'm happy to be there. Oh, and by the way, I need half your paycheck at the end of the month. So go ahead, and I'll give you my bank details and—" He cut me off, unsure what I was talking about. "Well, if you want me to come and do your job, you'll have to pay me," I replied. "Look, you're experienced at this. Are you telling me you cannot hire the best assistant manager in your area?"

He explained that, in the past, his previous managers always wanted to be there during the interview process. In other words, his previous managers didn't trust him enough to do his job. He wasn't given the authority to succeed, and he was unfairly held accountable for the performance of the personnel his boss hired. I imagine he led his team with a similar outlook.

"No," I said. "I want to give you full credit for your success and hold you accountable for failures, so hire the best person you can, and if it doesn't work, I'm going to ask you what went wrong and how you'll fix it. Better yet, why don't you get the actual branch manager to hire their assistant? Wouldn't that make more sense, letting her choose her own team?" He couldn't believe what I was saying. For years, he'd been operating in a system where the boss had to oversee every decision and had the ultimate final say. He was an A player, but his bosses had relegated him to a B player. This is true for many businesses, and it stems from an outdated mindset that holds true leadership back.

A players help A players thrive.
B players control C players.

The objective in every company needs to be about unleashing the talent inside the organization, where there are likely individuals ready to break free and fulfill their potential. Yet for so long, they've been held back with bureaucracy, micromanagement, targets rather than goals, and a culture that seeks to give those above control over those below. This new approach to connected leadership unleashes talent that is inherently driven. This is about inspiring rather than controlling, which creates real impact from the leadership rather than the illusion of impact through command and control.

REFLECTIVE EXERCISE

1. Who are the smartest employees in your organization? List them below. Are they the leaders or the employees?

_____

_____

_____

_____

_____

_____

2. Who are the A players in your organization? And the B players? Write in the major names below that fit into either category. What changes can be made to help the B players eventually become A players?

_____

_____

_____

_____

_____

_____

_____

3. Given the centralized role of recruiting/hiring, how can the process be adapted to allow your managers to select the best fits for their team?

_____

_____

_____

_____

_____

_____

SUMMARY/KEY TAKEAWAYS

Empowering people through inspiring leadership creates a culture where everyone seeks to be the best in the world at their job. Often, where things begin to fall apart is when key talents don't have the authority to create their own team yet are held responsible for their performance. There are definite benefits to having centralized experts in recruiting and hiring, but ultimately, decisions for selecting new hires need to be made by the team leader.

And, in turn, that team leader needs to have the skill, confidence, and support to make their call on who best fits and then be held accountable for the result. And it crucially requires support from that manager's manager to allow them to make those decisions. This also requires learning on the job as wisdom is only gained by experience, not classroom training. Once someone has worked in an environment where there is no authority to hire, yet they're held accountable, they are reluctant to take a risk or make the call. This does not allow for the manager to grow into a more effective leader nor does the organization benefit from this manager's full capability.

16

SETTING ASPIRATIONAL GOALS

"We aim above the mark to hit the mark."
– Ralph Waldo Emerson

I've always wanted people to own their roles and responsibilities. A lot of it comes from me simply not wanting to spend my time monitoring grown adults to do what they were supposed to do. I would much rather spend my time developing a greater understanding of how to support their development and success. Monitoring feels tactical whereas focusing on the ecosystem to encourage higher performance is more strategic. And creating a high-performance culture should be the primary job of any leader. However, there is an important part of the business cycle that can subtly undermine the performance of a team and redefine the culture without anyone taking notice: the planning cycle.

One of the most important functions of a manager is to create a plan and set out the subjective and objective expectations for each person to ensure successful outcomes, such as meeting the budgets, which typically includes setting targets. Although it may seem merely semantic, there is an important nuance between setting targets and setting goals. Setting a target gives someone a number to reach for, but in a budget mindset, you're consciously telling them that this is the number they should put their focus on, no more, no less. But what if they could achieve more than that? What if, on reflection, that initial target is far too small? This focus on hitting targets and budgets creates undesirable situations like when a salesperson meets their quarterly target or quota in the first couple of weeks, then slacks off the rest of the quarter or holds back orders for the next quarter. The same attitude occurs when there is a surplus of money left in a budget that needs to be spent in order to keep the same budget in the next cycle, known as "Use it or lose it." These examples and others encourage behaviors that go against the notion of high performance and put the focus on high conformance. To change the mindset that led to these limiting behaviors, we used a simple, but effective mentality.

The budget or target mentality is just like that of a high jumper. The bar represents the target, and the high jumper only spends the amount of energy necessary to clear the bar. A high jumper will clear the bar by a few inches each time that bar is raised. What we wanted to do was to create the mindset of a sprinter. A sprinter steps up to the line and gives themselves permission to go all out to outperform their competition on their left and right. They may have a goal in mind, but they perform all out in their attempt to win the race. We changed the word targets to goals to underscore the mindset we wanted our teams to bring to work every day.

Of course, the company needs to know what to expect and communicate regarding the financial performance. Overly ambitious goals that aren't met can result in analysts panning management for missed projections, but goals are a far more effective way to communicate expectations because they can be set at three different levels for three different purposes: minimum, expected, and stretch. Minimum goals are set to communicate the minimum requirement to keep a job. Expected goals are the company's performance expectations, internally and externally. Stretch goals are designed to focus on a higher ceiling as an aspirational objective that inspires individuals and teams to stretch as high as they can go. It's a slight change in philosophy, yet it creates a fundamental shift in mindset. We developed this stretch mindset by first asking managers what they thought their fair share of the market was for every product and second. "If everything went perfectly for you this year, what do you think you could do?" Instead of giving each of our 1,800 branch managers a centrally developed plan and a set of targets, we gave them information about their historical performance, their share of the market, their customers, the competition, and the products. We asked them to review this information, provide their unique insights, and consider what they thought was possible. From there, we encouraged them to work with their team to create their own aspirational individual goals, plans, and other supporting actions.

We didn't know how this would work the first time we tried it, but we felt that since we were building our cultural transformation on the values of mutual trust and respect, our teams would step up and make the shift. We wanted to turn away from the budget mentality. Instead of negotiating and managing targets to keep expectations of the executive team low, we wanted "business owners" to consider what was possible based on their knowledge of their capabilities and the marketplace. This change also eliminated incremental thinking from central teams and executives. Typically, goals are negotiated based on the last period's performance, rather than what could be possible. A manager who had underperformed from their potential saying that they could do a 15 percent uplift on a poor number wasn't going to fly. If their fair share was 75 percent higher than the last period's performance, I wanted this number to be their stretch goal. We had to do this while assuring the managers that they would be held accountable for hitting their expected goal, not the stretch goals. However, they would benefit financially from achieving that higher number. This created a fundamental shift in mindset and pushed managers to entirely new levels of production.

It's difficult to hand over so much control and trust so many different departments and people. But remember, the primary role of a leader is to get the best out of everyone. Their job is to help their organization grow and move toward success in its vision. It also forces those inside the organization—at all levels of the hierarchy—to step up and reevaluate their role in the business. It's at this stage that highly talented individuals—who have been buried in the company—are discovered. Be it through creativity, innovation, productivity, or work ethic, stars rise to the top. It's not always necessary to look outside the organization for new hires because the best hires are already there.

Of course, many managers felt uncomfortable with this much authority or were not skilled enough to complete their market plan. We held special training sessions for these managers and, during that first year, were more hands-on in helping to create the plans. Not the numbers, mind you— the plans. They all created their own goals, which was crucial. The results surprised many in the finance department to whom the concepts of delegating goal setting and setting stretch goals were foreign. The roll-up of the goals from the branches significantly exceeded the corporate targets and, more importantly, because the managers created their own success plans for the year, they had taken ownership of these goals. As if by magic, this planning process led us to not only set higher targets than the company expected, but we ended up hitting the collective stretch goals for the year, which were 140 percent to plan. This was an organization that was a dismal 48 percent to plan when the *Whistleblower* program aired.

It's a powerful shift that transforms the mindset of those in the organization. This must begin with the leader, who sets the tone. They need to let go of control, replace it with trust, and communicate to those around them as adults capable of running their business. This is where we turn our attention next: the role that communication plays to inform everyone of the journey and progress along the way.

REFLECTIVE EXERCISE

1. Does the budgeting process affect your organization's performance? Does it create a tighter connection to the vision statement or a sense of separation?

_____

_____

_____

_____

_____

2. Have you experienced setting target and stretch goals? If so, what was the impact on your performance?

_____

_____

_____

_____

_____

SUMMARY/KEY TAKEAWAYS

It's very common for organizations, especially larger, established players, to think about their business and planning cycle with a budget mentality. This is obviously done because investors or stock analysts who represent investors, need predictability of results. CEOs also need to have a tight rein on key financial ratios, of which controlling costs are a common and integral piece. This effects the planning cycles and creates the need for limits, or budgets, on where money is spent in order to have control over these costs. While this is fairly straightforward and logical, what is not always appreciated is that this approach to planning creates a mindset inside the organization that drives behaviors that are limited by definition and can be contrary to the aspirations in the organization's vision statement, which are designed and communicated to build excitement for what's possible and create emotional attachment to the potential of the organization. Ultimately, the budget mindset has a far greater effect as it impacts the culture much more than the annual reminder of the aspirational vision.

Leaders who are courageous enough to think aspirationally can break the budget mindset prevalent in so many organizations, destroying the self-limiting beliefs of the budget mindset, and unleash the truth that higher performance—much higher performance—is within their grasp.

17

CONNECTED LEADERSHIP

"The way I think about culture is that modern
humans have radically changed the way that they
work and the way that they live. Companies need
to change the way they manage and lead to match
the way modern humans actually work and live."
– Brian Halligan, CEO, Hubspot

This shift to empower colleagues throughout the organization began to foster a level of trust that didn't exist before.
I began to get suggestions from employees that had great
benefit to the company. Not only did they understand
and accept the challenges, but they embraced the change.
Changing the old narrative is part of the power shift toward
connected leadership. Communication began to reflect this
unified and aligned approach to running the business, rather
than trying to hide the truth. We shared the challenges and
opportunities in ways that enlisted everyone to the cause.

Just as we were getting our arms around the transformation
and performance was picking up across the board, the financial crisis began to take shape in 2008. Although the timing

was terrible for us, we had to react rapidly, make some tough decisions, and change all our plans. But the values and principles we had set out had to remain the same. In fact, they were more important than ever.

I'll always remember our monthly business review with the global head of corporate and retail banking who fully embraced the command-and-control style of management. He loved to create stress and discomfort in the belief that it would push managers to work harder, try harder, and go further than they would have otherwise. Although it wasn't my style of management or the style of my boss—the UK CEO—it was important to be responsive to show him that we were on top of things, even if we did things differently.

This meeting was on a Wednesday evening. True to his style, he wanted to give me an impossible task with an impossible timeframe in the hopes that even if I failed, the effort of trying to succeed would propel me to a higher level of accomplishment than I would have achieved without his intervention. In his directive style of speaking, he told me, "Mike, you have 80 percent (30,000 full-time equivalent) of the company's workforce in our largest part of the business working for you. This financial crisis is going to be very bad. With the way it's unfolding, it's important that we cut costs aggressively. And since most costs are related to people, I have personally run the numbers and have determined that you will need to reduce staffing by 1,200 FTE. And I mean actual staff reductions, not hiring freezes or vague plans that don't really cut costs. I want actual names on a report in my email by Monday night. Do you have any questions?" My response was quick. "No, that makes sense, and I will have this for you by Sunday, not Monday." He said, "Are you sure? Maybe you need some of my staff to help you do this because I am serious. I will now expect these names by Sunday. I will be waiting for them." I told him, "Nope. I don't need any help. I'm on it and will be ready."

There was nothing wrong with this request because it was absolutely necessary. We had to react to the bigger picture and adjust our costs to meet these severe challenges. Yet, in issuing the challenge in such a condescending manner— built on the assumption that I was unaware of the severity of the crisis unfolding—he appeared almost smug. He believed I would spend the next few days in a blind panic.

But I didn't panic. I already had a list of over 2,000 names prepared that I had gathered over the previous two weeks. Rather than project his style of management onto my team, I had tapped into the goodwill created by the changes I've described earlier in this book and had already approached my senior leaders about the upcoming looming crisis. Speaking adult-to-adult, I gave them context. "Our finance team believes revenues are going to shrink significantly, so we need to shrink our cost base accordingly. I need each of you to look at your business units and consider how the crisis will affect your business and where you can cut costs. Don't worry about what you can't control, such as leases and utilities, but look at your staffing, training, travel, and general spending. Give me ideas of where we can cut costs, especially staffing."

I was honest with them. I encouraged them to ask me questions, and I answered them as best as I could. But I learned a lot from them as they had valuable context about their businesses that exceeded my knowledge. They also gave me their thoughtful analysis of several challenges we faced and educated me on the finer points, including political and regulatory pressures. We spoke openly and transparently. No Jedi mind games, no tricks, no battle for control. It was so well understood by everyone that they came back to me with that list of over 2,000 names, as well as other ideas on where we could cut costs—totaling several hundred million pounds.

By the time I submitted my list—on Saturday night, by the way, not Sunday—we had already vetted the plans with the unions, a crucial step that would have fallen through the cracks if I had waited for the directive to tackle this problem in the timeline demanded. Where other banks fell foul to the unions and their subsequent legal challenges and complaints, not to mention unflattering articles about brutal staffing cuts, ours was the only major UK bank that didn't have a complaint from the union or negative press. And it all began by building an uncommon connection with my team and tapping into the mutual trust and respect we held for each other. My team stepped up and amazed that executive with their willingness to do the difficult thing—but the right thing—in ways that made me proud to work in the organization.

Building trust and respect between everyone in the company and communicating in ways that magnify this connection is a crucial role of leadership, and I'm certain it doesn't happen consistently. The key question to consider is: Does communication center around the assumption that the employees need to have "managed" information, carefully crafted, and homogenized to avoid any legal challenge or a myriad of other risks? Of course, there needs to be caution in sharing information with such diverse groups of people, but this example shows that it's possible to manage those risks without losing the company's soul and creating a greater divide between management and everyone else.

A leader's voice, in word and deed, is a keystone of the culture. It is difficult to create a trusting, functional, high-performing culture, but it can be eroded quite easily when communication doesn't align with the stated values of the company.

In his last letter to shareholders, Jack Welch references this exact point:

> We made our greatest leap forward when we began removing our Type Four managers (those that deliver stellar results but don't share the company values) and made it clear to the entire company why they were asked to leave, not the usual personal reasons or to pursue other opportunities but for not sharing our values. Until an organization develops the courage to do this, people will never have full confidence that these soft values are real. There are undoubtedly a few Type Fours remaining, and they must be found. They must leave the company because their behavior weakens the trust that more than 300,000 people have in this leadership.

Aligning the strategy with the purpose, supported by values that inform all forms of communication and are consistently on display, is the crucial formula to creating a functional, intentional culture based on trust and empowerment throughout the organization.

REFLECTIVE EXERCISE

1. As a manager/leader in your organization, which do you spend more time doing: monitoring your team's performance or growing their capabilities (and why)?

_____

_____

_____

_____

_____

2. Does your organization have any "Type Fours"? If so, how does the leadership deal with them?

_____

_____

_____

_____

3. What are your views on the communications from your organization? Do you think they align with the corporate values, or do they create a division between what's said and what's done?

_____

_____

_____

_____

SUMMARY/KEY TAKEAWAYS

Once the leader has set the stage by creating an environment of empowerment, true accountability, and mutual trust, it's vital to sustain that through thoughtful communications. All communications must reflect the leader's commitment to practicing the organization's values or the leader faces the risk of looking hypocritical. It's a fine balance, to be sure, as there are definitely times when full disclosure would open the organization up to risks it would like to avoid, but overly engineered PR-driven communications that are so opaque as to be meaningless come across as disingenuous. Holding employees accountable for demonstrating the corporate values, while not holding the organization to the same standard is sowing the seeds of discord.

The solution is to adopt adult-to-adult communications that authentically reflect the values of the company while providing important context to the issues discussed. One of the key roles a leader plays is communicator, and a culture built around adult-to-adult communications empowers them to be powerful messengers.

18

THE BARRIERS TO CONNECTED LEADERSHIP

"Your path is not to seek for love, but merely
to seek and find all the barriers within yourself that you
have built against it."
– Rumi

By committing yourself to becoming a more connected leader, you can become more relevant and have much greater impact on today's multi-generational, multicultural, and hyper-connected world. This different way to lead will create success many times greater than the results most managers create when they continue to put the finances of the company first. And since the core of any strategy is differentiation, it's this difference in leadership perspective that creates opportunities.

However, those who want to create a different level of success but are unwilling to change how they view their role as a leader will always face an uphill battle. Some of the barriers to adapting to this model are unique to each situation, but some of them are predictable. Some of them arise regardless of business or a particular crisis.

This is how we need to end this section on leadership, discussing the barriers faced during this power shift toward connected, more empathetic leadership.

Barrier One: Siloed managers defending their team and their turf.
Solution: The Team One concept.

In *The Five Dysfunctions of a Team*, Patrick Lencioni focuses on the five things a team needs to function properly. Let me explain the issue: Organizations create functional structures (aka divisions, an apropos name) at the executive level to divide the work around the expertise of each executive. It's quite common and reasonable that executives first consider the impact on their team when discussing key business decisions with their counterparts. This is how politicians are expected to behave and is quite common in organizations. However, various dysfunctions develop when this behavior is prevalent, such as different divisions launching competing initiatives, a lack of communication between departments, and sacrificing the customer experience by creating programs with a benefit to one's own team.

As we were creating our transformation plan at Barclays, siloed thinking was a major issue that greatly contributed to the cultural dysfunction. As Lencioni points out, the five things that need to be present for a team to be truly functional were largely absent. Each of these dysfunctions builds upon the next. They are:

> **Trust:** A team that does not work together has an inherent absence of trust. But to build trust, you must have…

Conflict: A team needs to have conflict because if you don't have open conflict, you don't have transparent conversations, which are crucial to establish trust. Eliminating passive-aggressive behaviors creates trust that everyone has the same objectives and that all teammates are being open and honest with any concerns. This opens the door for developing...

Commitment: A team needs to be committed toward a common goal (or direction). This is the collective energy that allows organizations and teams to stay the course when the outcome is in doubt.

Without commitment, a team cannot work together in unity. The keyword is that the goal is *common*; uniting around a shared purpose is what powers the team, which then embraces...

Accountability: A team needs to be able to hold each other accountable. Otherwise, those in the team will struggle to work alongside one another if it's perceived that someone is not pulling their weight. As we've already discussed, aligning accountability with responsibility and appropriate authority creates an outcome-driven team, producing...

Results: A team needs to clearly understand what winning looks like and measure progress toward that goal relentlessly. This is the only way to create an evolving, learning, high-performing team that produces the necessary results, across the entire scorecard, including financial success. This is how the ROI of a culture is determined; ROI is the ultimate scorecard for measuring success.

This is how these dysfunctions showed up at Barclays: There were disconnected product campaigns in each product area trying to shout loudest for the customer's attention. There were also various incentives available to the sales teams for success in selling each product. In short, every executive was focused on their team's objectives and results rather than concerning themselves with the bigger picture. Our customer-facing areas were awash in multiple, disconnected campaigns with various themes, color schemes, and offers. At an offsite retreat for my executive team, we discussed the creation of a framework of interdependencies and broke down the barriers—caused by "constituent thinking"—that put an executive's functional team needs above other outcomes. We labeled the new approach Team One, which was to begin looking at *each other* as the team, not our constituents. We committed to serving the collective needs of our new Team One, and we began building a deeper appreciation for each other's challenges, perspectives, and expertise. We started by building trust through difficult conversations and ended with an aligned plan with shared goals and incentives tied to Team One success, which, of course, was to achieve our collective vision.

This played a huge role in the overall success of the organization. If we had left the existing leadership fundamentals and silos in place, we could have hired the best people and launched the best products with the best advertising, but with very little effect due to the dysfunctional environment. It would have been like transplanting palm trees in Alaska. Regardless of the health and quality of the tree, it cannot survive in that ecosystem. Even the best-laid plans and top talent would be sabotaged by poor leadership practices. If we didn't change our perspective at the top, nothing else would matter.

Barrier Two: Decision making on an island.
Solution: Data-driven, team approach to decisions.

Every organization and leader has a certain decision-making style. Too often, this involves one person being presented with a problem and making the call on what they think is the best solution. The challenge in a fast-paced organization is that often this precludes a proper root cause analysis, gathering data and analyzing it to derive insights, then exploring various solutions before making the decision. Of course, this works fine for small, routine issues, but the problem is that it becomes the go-to style for all decisions, leaving potentially superior options unidentified. This process enabled the walls of the silos to be hardened as each executive made the key decisions for their teams in isolation.

In order to activate our Team One approach, we transformed how our teams worked by playing a simple game called the Survival Game. Each team member gets a survival scenario, such as a plane crashing on a desert island or in the mountains. They are given a list of all the items available that survived the crash, and their challenge is to choose the ten items, in order, that they would keep, giving themselves the best chance to survive. Each executive had to complete the challenge on their own and make their lists independent of any other feedback. The results were to be scored based on the alignment with the correct actions by experts.

There was a wide array of skills and experience represented on the team, from people who had been in the military to others who had never been camping, so scores were all over the board. Before sharing the answers to the challenge from the team of survival experts, we grouped the executives into small teams and asked them to collaborate and come up with their team responses. Collaboration differs from compromise, which was instructive in helping the teams reach conclusions that they could all stand behind.

The fascinating thing is that the teams scored higher than even the highest-performing individual in every case. Even more surprisingly, one of the biggest contributors to the team's success was that the highest-scoring teams chose their facilitator on factors other than perceived expertise, which would seem counterintuitive. But by choosing the best person to lead based on their ability to organize and lead discussions, they created a true team approach that involved the collective rather than one dominant perspective overriding the others. As many of the executives previously believed that decisions are best left to the most senior person, and that team decision-making created groupthink and bureaucratic blockages, this exercise was eye-opening for them.

The key was collaboration, not negotiation or compromise. This simple exercise set the stage for the group to work much more effectively on things like setting priorities for the £700 million budget for investing in the infrastructure, product launch protocol, and product marketing planning. I knew we had arrived at a functioning Team One when executives, working as a group, agreed to put another team's project above their own.

Besides becoming a tremendous decision-making team, they started to connect on a personal level, spending more time together socially. Even today, on our quarterly reunion video calls, the stories Team One tells are about these social gatherings rather than our financial success as a company, even though every single executive is proud of the results we achieved, and over half have gone on to become CEOs themselves.

While the game is quite simplistic, just doing the exercise itself does not create change. The important takeaway was that decision-making can be a team process, and we formalized the process by always beginning with a root cause analysis, driven by information and data rather than jumping to solutions based on intuition alone. I'm sure most companies think they have a similar process, and if they do, that's great. But I am shocked at how many teams I speak to bow to the leader or subject matter expert's intuition rather than seek full understanding of an issue before deciding the course of action.

I like analogies, so here's another one–this is like having a group of people decide to go on vacation. Everyone begins calling out where they want to go, essentially throwing solution darts at a problem. This is classic group dynamics at work and can lead to great frustration, not to mention a total lack of progress. An alternative approach would be to decide whether they wanted to travel near or far, cold weather or hot weather, drive or fly, etc. Now, it's not a big deal when we're just talking about taking a trip, but it is a big deal when solving a business issue.

A-to-B decision-making does not produce the best results because not all potential solutions are vetted. For example, where one executive might say we need better frontline staff training, another might say we need faster, more reliable systems. A third might want to dismiss the issue altogether because the call volume was a temporary spike and won't be sustained. This is chaotic and inefficient, leading to the loudest voice driving their solution or, worse yet, a compromised decision. Instead, we developed the discipline to do the commonsense thing and collect data, analyze the findings, then discuss several possible solutions, vetting them and thus landing on the right one through collaboration.

I will repeat that this sounds like an obvious process to follow, but to many, it feels unnecessarily time-consuming and bureaucratic, so it's easy to get caught up in pressing for the speediest resolution or looking only for the limited data that supports the favorite recommended solution.

Besides creating sub-optimal outcomes, this can be a dangerous step in suppressing the creativity that could result in more successful ways to solve the problem.

Barrier Three: A sense of entitlement.
Solution: A sense of accountability to the customer.

Throughout my career, my personal success has always been closely linked to overseeing the customer journey. As such, I've always felt a sense of responsibility to the customer and the customer-facing staff. If they are happy, I can be happy. If they are not, I cannot. If our results are positive, I'm doing my job. If not, I'm not. But it was natural for me to think this way because I had always worked with the people who worked directly with the customers.

In our transformation of the UK Retail Bank, I wanted to emphasize this necessary connection to the customer, so I labeled our transformation program at Barclays "Real Retail." "Real" as in genuine. Transformation was really going to happen—not another "This, too, shall pass" campaign. "Retail" because all retail organizations are, or should be, fundamentally customer-centric. They don't need to declare it; it's in their DNA. As we began to gain traction with our customer advocacy scores, the support areas began to take notice. As I've mentioned before, the buzz from the frontline was noticeable, and I was frequently asked by those in support roles outside my organization about Real Retail and how it was driving a noticeably higher metabolic rate in what had been a habitually underperforming part of the organization. Based on their questions, it was clear the notion of customer-centricity didn't necessarily seem to fit the definition of their role, their focus, or even how their effectiveness was measured and rewarded.

One day, I was invited to attend a meeting of several of these support department managers from operations, technology, and finance who asked how they could adapt Real Retail in their departments since they weren't customer-facing. It was a good question.

I asked them if they had customers, and they said yes—they treat the areas they support as internal customers. My response, intending to be a bit provocative, was that the difference between them and the frontline was their sense of entitlement. Somewhat taken aback, they asked what I meant by that, so I pointed out that their customers couldn't fire them if they didn't like their service. And they knew this. While they called them customers, they really viewed them as a captive audience that they supported—within parameters that they defined or negotiated.

This wasn't to say they didn't care or share the same passion for doing their part to help the organization fulfill its mission. Far from it. These were true professionals in their areas, passionate about Barclays' success and balancing numerous daily demands on their limited resources. These demands on their resources led to the creation of Service Level Agreements (SLAs)—which are designed to inform the departments they support what level of service they can expect. They're a form of commitment by the support area on things like response times on service requests but are also helpful if there are service complaints or even unrealistic demands by their "customers" that create disagreements later. Fulfilling the timeline in the service requests is a key determinant in the support areas' key performance indicators (KPIs) and bonuses. This is not illogical nor is it inherently a bad thing, but it creates a separation of objectives because the frontline is driven by the external customer's timelines, which may not agree or align with our internally negotiated SLAs. They may file complaints or take their business elsewhere, which naturally affects the frontline employees' KPIs.

They asked what could be done about this, as the focus of the various groups is necessarily different. My response was that this is a mindset issue. If they could begin thinking of their function or support area differently, they could apply the Real Retail mindset as well. After they focused on creating a world-class support area, what if they visualized that they were so proficient that they could outsource their services to other organizations for a fee? What would it take to think of their departments this way? How would this shift their mindset from being a cost center with SLA targets to a revenue center with aspirational goals of winning the business from their external clients?

Well, it would take benchmarking service levels at other similar organizations around the world, gathering direct feedback from internal customers on what it would take to delight (exceeding SLA expectations) them, gathering testimonials, rethinking their goal setting to have more objective measures, and even reconsidering incentive plans around these objective measures. In other words, they needed to look at their areas as stand-alone businesses and develop the mindset of a startup.

While this was merely an intellectual exercise in redefining their perspective of the service they provided, their response was heartwarming! It supported my earlier contention that, by and large, the vast majority of people are trying to do a good job and contribute meaningfully. To do so, leaders must adopt a different mindset around the relevance of their role within the broader context of the business. When these managers saw a different way to view their valuable contribution, it changed their mindset around their function and created a stronger connection between the various teams.

Addressing these three barriers with a connected, aligned leadership team creates opportunities to unleash performance throughout the organization that will redefine productivity limits through ever-higher employee engagement. By addressing the basic relevance of leadership and challenging them to rethink their role and who they served, we were starting to build the transformation plan that would guide the entire organization in this new journey. We just had to do it such that every one of the 30,000 employees understood what we were going to change, why we had to change, and how they would contribute.

REFLECTIVE EXERCISE

1. As a manager/leader within your organization, what barriers do you face to more deeply connect with your team?

_____

_____

_____

_____

2. What changes can be made to have your organization better identify different departments to fit into a Team-One concept?

_____

_____

_____

_____

_____

3. What common goals needs to be set to get your team to succeed together?

_____

_____

_____

_____

SUMMARY/KEY TAKEAWAYS

It's important to understand the barriers to creating a collaborative, functional, and conscious culture. I've identified three, which are siloed executives, disparate decision making, and entitlement. These three barriers must be addressed, or any cultural transformation will be deeply undermined and unsustainable. In this chapter, I shared how we actively called out that these barriers, or behaviors, would keep us from making meaningful improvements in our performance and, therefore, our vision would be unattainable. The methods shared are incredibly simplistic, but each allowed the executive to model the required change in behaviors necessary to begin collaborating and connecting in entirely new ways. The result was that we benefited from the full range of skills represented by the group of executives, and crucially, we sent the signal to the rest of the organization that the changes we were making were going to be embraced at all levels, thus eliminating the possibility that our collective voice would be perceived as hypocritical, which would have been the end to our cultural transformation.

What was also instructional was that we uncovered a sense of entitlement that needed to be redefined in order for the support areas to embrace and incorporate Real Retail. By redefining the way these support areas defined their roles, we unleashed the same discretionary energy that permeated the customer-facing teams.

19

WHY YOU NEED A RALLYING CALL

"If you're good to your staff when things are going well,
they'll rally when times go bad."
– Mary Kay Ash, Founder, Mary Kay Cosmetics

We wanted to create an entirely different culture that would bring clarity and authenticity to our common purpose. This was nothing short of a movement, and every movement needs a call to action that creates an emotional urge to turn away from something undesirable and turn toward the desired outcome. We wanted everyone on the team to know that real change was possible. And as it turned out, we were essentially pushing on an open door.

A movement often begins at a low point when it becomes clear that things cannot continue as they have been—when people can no longer make do with what's in front of them. Without this catalyst, there is little motivation to change. You can cognitively acknowledge that things need to change, but it's difficult to take any real, sustainable action. There may be a desire, but there's no commitment. Diet trends are built on this realization. But once this trigger—*whether it's caused by a crisis or a person*—forces you to see the problem, it's impossible to unsee.

Real, meaningful change requires passion. The passion for creating a new reality must exceed the emotion that keeps the organization grounded in the current reality. This is why well-intended campaigns designed to create a new reality will ultimately fail unless they are passionately sponsored from the top and garner commitment from everyone in the organization.

But motivation alone isn't enough. As I've said, real change begins with a leader who is willing to be the voice of change and communicate a journey that every single person can understand and get on board with. This leader needs to garner trust for everyone to sustain the desire to succeed.

I still recall describing Real Retail in a meeting with a large group of managers. Afterward, two managers approached me, and the more experienced manager said, "We have seen so many programs over the past five years, none of which created a meaningful impact. But we believe in you and what your team is doing. We just want you to know that." I can't tell you how valuable that validation was. Without creating this belief, Real Retail would have been another in the series of failed transformations, or more accurately, campaigns. Any leader wanting to turn a dysfunctional culture around must understand that it's more than a change dictated from the top. It must be holistic in nature, and the new reality needs to be a reality that everyone can believe in—but even then, there will be resistance. Every situation is different and unique; the larger the organization, the more complex this process becomes. The team will undoubtedly uncover bigger issues than they could have imagined, but it's the conviction to change that will see them through.

So far, the discussion has been about setting the table with key philosophies and principles and making the case for fundamental change. Now, I'd like to turn our attention to the transformation plan itself, where the focus is on the journey and the psychology behind each component. For many leaders I speak to, this is where they want to begin, but I've deliberately saved this for the last section of the book because without the information I've shared so far, the process that follows simply will not be sufficient to drive cultural transformation.

I am confident that this guide not only provides the impetus to create an effective change program but goes further, helping to create a bit of magic that results from discovering the company's soul.

REFLECTIVE EXERCISE

1. What internal "dysfunction" needs to be addressed by senior management to get all to buy in to the movement?

_____

_____

_____

_____

2. What bigger issues have been, or may be uncovered to resolve before you can get complete organizational buy-in?

_____

_____

_____

_____

_____

_____

_____

_____

_____

_____

SUMMARY/KEY TAKEAWAYS

Organizations in crisis need to view this as a gift that provides incentive to change. Often, these changes that need to happen were prevalent earlier, but were ignored for any variety of reasons. In speaking recently with the head of strategy for a growing company, she expressed deep frustration that the CEO ignored her calls for crucial changes in order to remain ahead of competitors. In the same conversation, the head of innovation at a global organization said that leadership ignored the threat posed by non-traditional competitors. In both cases, there is genuine concern that a crisis awaits if the warnings are ignored.

Unfortunately, it's the crisis that provides the impetus for a fundamental review of the factors that lead to the crisis and the realization that nothing less than a rallying cry will produce the energy and motivation for meaningful cultural change.

20

THE JOURNEY TO A HIGH-PERFORMING CULTURE

"High expectations and belief in people
leads to high performance."
– Paul Hersey, Behavioral Scientist,
Author of *Situational Leadership*

To transform from an undesirable culture to a high-performing, intentional, and aligned culture, there are five distinct steps your organization must take.

STEP ONE: DEVELOP INSIGHTS AND ANALYTICS

The first stage of the transformation journey is to develop insights and analytics on customers and employees. While I've explained the need to do this and the various methods we used, the key point here is to use this as a baseline for the steps that follow, including communications strategies, prioritizing the workflows, and determining where to invest to reflect feedback on the challenges in the current environment. There are two areas of impact to understand in order to create the case for change: employees and customers. Knowing the impact on each is the crucial first step.

The Impact on the Employee:

You will never find the answers you need by sitting in a boardroom doing a desktop review of the business. This is true in any business but especially for a business that has lost its way. The goal is to rediscover the soul of the business, and to do this, you need to speak to the heart. The heart of the business is the front line, whether that front line is working directly with external customers or support areas, or working directly with internal customers. These colleagues understand the pain points in broken processes and the things the company does that makes serving their customers harder. Instead of digging into the reports and numbers to find answers, a leader and their team needs to get on the shop floor to hear what's really going on.

In order to gather the best, most authentic information about what needs to change, the visits must be in person to create a higher level of trust with the employees and there must be a genuine desire to listen and commit to addressing the most valid points. This is why suggestion boxes, electronic or not, have little impact. When nothing happens with most suggestions, after a while, employees give up and stop trying to think innovatively or sharing their perspectives altogether.

Please know that when I'm discussing executive field visits, I am not talking about those carefully engineered visits where everything is set up to make the best impression on the boss, and only the top performers can share suggestions. I'm talking about creating opportunities for open, direct, and honest conversations with a cross-section of the employee base that has vital information on the ecosystem.

Now, not all feedback is actionable and all of it certainly needs to be validated, but this is about gathering information and data, which is separate from the process of implementing solutions. But even if a suggestion is not ultimately followed, it's important to provide follow-up information for why it wasn't done. Trust is not built by executing the suggestion. It's built by listening and considering the suggestion in a thoughtful way, then communicating the rationale for the final decision.

In our case, the BBC had given us a good idea of what was actually going on, but I had a feeling there was a lot more to the story. So, my team and I used the connections and trust we had built to good use, got on the train, and started to visit branches around the UK. What I learned was astounding.

For example, on one of my visits, I traveled to a branch in York and met with a woman who had worked as a cashier at Barclays for thirty-two years. "I started here when I was sixteen," she told me, "and this is the first time I've met the person in your job."

That hit me hard. She had spent three decades at the organization and never met an executive. As you can imagine, she had a lot to tell me. I listened as she vented about how she was continually sent into sales training courses to boost her success, even though she hated to sell. "I'm always top in service, but the lowest performer in sales, Mike," she said. "I hate to sell."

I could see the pain in her face. She felt like she was letting the organization down, and it made her feel like she wasn't good at her job—all because we kept trying to force her into doing something she clearly didn't feel comfortable doing. At the same time, this was a key requirement for her role. My conversation with her was not about how to learn to sell, but more about how to redefine what selling meant as she viewed selling as what a used car salesperson does. We discussed how, in this context, selling means making sure that her customers knew how we could help them make more money or save them more money. We didn't want her to get them to do something we wanted them to do, merely inform them of all our relevant products and services as an extension of providing the level of customer care she was famous for.

I knew I could learn a lot from this woman because there was no doubt that many others faced this same quandary, so I invited her to the main office in Canary Wharf, London. Her face lit up as she asked, "Can I bring my husband? He works at Barclays as well. We started at the same time and have been together ever since. We want to see the head office for the first time!"

I couldn't believe it. Between her and her husband, they had worked at Barclays for sixty-four years! During that time, they had never visited the central office. They never met their executives. They had to participate in various training and seminars about something deeply uncomfortable to them. In my mind, this was a failure by the organization because, in our desire to drive better sales, we didn't take the time to consider how we could accomplish the company's objectives and stay within the value sets of these two long-time employees.

Connecting this to our broader challenge, this entire crisis came about because the BBC placed reporters in our call centers and branches, revealing a concerning push to drive sales at all costs, thereby creating opportunities to mis-sell. They opened our eyes to what was going on, which came as a surprise to everyone high up in the organization.

Executives think they know what's going on. They think they know what the problems are. But typically, it's the crisis that reveals that the culture—the ecosystem—is dysfunctional. Again, this is why it's essential to connect with the frontline staff and treat them as valuable employees with information every bit as valuable as that collected by the customer insights staff in the central office, not to mention the opportunity to show gratitude for decades of loyalty and hard work.

More revealing was when I brought this couple from York to our offices in Canary Wharf, I raised eyebrows because I wanted to use one of the executive conference rooms that we usually reserve for important clients and investors. It has furniture from the original Barclays building, which is 350 years old. That I wanted to use it so I could speak to a couple of branch employees raised a bit of a stir. But I was going to use it. And I planned to do it a lot more.

As word spread about these visits not just led by me, but primarily led by the head of the branch system who had worked with me at Washington Mutual and lived the same values, with a deep passion for putting people first, we began to create a valuable connection with the frontline staff. It's not enough to send out a survey and hope employees will complete it on their lunch break. Nor is it enough to have a conference call where the executive does all the speaking, followed by a few planted questions from their staff.

In order to speak to more of our colleagues and gain valuable information on the issues workers were facing, supporting the new view of managerial relevance—shifting from command and control to empowerment—we held several employee focus groups to discuss the *Whistleblower* program. My small but mighty team of change agents, plus my uber-talented HR business partner, led the discussions using a simple but ingenious way of constructively drawing out the employees' perspectives of the company. Avoiding the pitfalls of sending out yet another survey asking people what they thought of the company, they presented a deck of picture cards to various focus groups of employees and asked them to pick the ones that best described Barclays. Repeatedly, across the country, the same four cards were selected.

The first was a picture of a dartboard. When asked why this card was chosen, the staff responded that this was because this was the predominant theme: Hitting their targets. All communications with upper management was about business performance and, more specifically, their performance to their targets.

The second picture selected was a hillside in Greece with different shapes and colors of houses. The reason this was selected was because they viewed our organization structure as choc-a-block, leaving them wondering who worked for whom and how to incorporate the various marketing campaigns and product goals in their location, not to mention the challenges represented when trying to set appointments for the various investment, mortgage, and local business specialists. The organization had set the seemingly reasonable objective to create P&L responsibility for each executive, which meant that we had entirely redundant structures in each division. This was what set up the creation of the solos we discussed earlier. Each division or silo rolled out their own plans with no regard to how this all affected the brand messaging to the customers or the cultural messaging to the staff.

The third card selected was a picture of a clown. When asked why they chose a clown, they said that despite the challenges, they loved their teams and coworkers. These relationships were their safe haven from the stress and confusion caused by target-focused managers and confusing divisional hierarchies. It was a wonderful reminder that these employees went to work every day and genuinely desired to do their jobs well, while enjoying time spent with their colleagues. This was a crucial perspective to keep in mind when we planned the transformation.

The fourth card selected was the picture of a lion. This was fascinating because Barclays' symbol was an eagle. When asked about this, they said it was because they felt pride in the brand. They felt like they were part of something larger than themselves.

This was priceless information because the shared perspectives were consistent wherever the team went. This gave us insight on where to focus our early efforts and, more importantly, how to craft communications in ways that were relevant to everyone. Since management's new focus was less about hitting targets and more about supporting and empowering individuals, we were able to incorporate the employees' own words into the transformation plan—describing the current state and turning the energy toward the realization of our aspirational vision.

In sports team environments, focusing on the energy, attitudes, and underlying motivation—the so-called intangibles–of the team are vital contributors to the overall performance level and provide the impetus for leaders whose aim is to inspire the team to greater performance. Only in business—the ultimate team sport—is this viewed as nonconsequential to the point that it is discouraged. One time, just before leaving Washington Mutual, my boss told me that employee engagement and aspirational goals were fine, but we had to focus more on the real work to do. I couldn't disagree more. I think the real work begins with, and is informed by, these aspirations that create an emotional connection to the organization's vision.

Asking our team to define how they felt at work made it easy to determine their pain points and how to best motivate and inspire them in subsequent communications of the transformation journey.

The Impact on Customers:

When auditing your ecosystem, the second place to look for insights is, obviously, to the customers. This is nothing new. All companies collect customer feedback in some form or another and use it for product or service improvements. But when a crisis forces an assessment of the culture, a fresh look is needed. We had all these processes in place, but perhaps like a lot of organizations, most of the data was mined for commercial purposes, not to determine how well we were fulfilling our brand promise. In addition, budget constraints caused by financial underperformance delayed many of the much-needed investment into improving the customer experience.

After the crisis, all this changed. Our COO, whose passionate dedication to the customer experience was unparalleled, began a process of gathering feedback through surveys, in-person focus groups, and even in-home observations. In essence, we were auditing our ability to be relevant in our customers' financial lives. This return to the fundamentals of the business required new approaches to gathering insights and new responses to the information received.

To say this was an eye-opening experience is an understatement. We found that what our customers said was totally aligned with what our frontline staff was saying. They brought fresh questions to the table, ones we never thought to ask. They told us how they felt, not just in the present, but previous frustrations they'd had when they'd tried to speak to Barclays in the past.

One incredibly valuable source of customer insights was the complaint logs. Not to overstate the obvious but digging into the complaints proved enormously helpful in helping us identify the root cause of the complaints, rather than merely correcting the specific complaint. A key metric was solving problems within a set timeframe, but in the course of running the business day to day, there had never been a concerted effort to analyze the issues more deeply. There is an adage about a person walking by a river who sees someone being swept downriver by the current yelling for help. The person jumps in and saves the drowning person, but then another one comes, then another, and another. Someone on shore asks every bystander to form a human chain to pull these people from the water and one person responds, "You go ahead and do that. But why don't we send someone upstream to see who's throwing these people in?" So, while we had a world-class complaint handling team, we…. the executives…had not considered looking upstream to understand the root causes.

Another way to view complaints is with appreciation. Our customers took the time to share how we had let them down and gave us the opportunity to remedy the situation. Many times, the relationship with the customer can be strengthened and expanded when the complaint is handled with proper care and urgency.

Furthermore, these complaint logs contained incredibly valuable data. It's obviously very difficult to solve all issues in a large organization on one go, so our COO set about identifying the top three complaints and the impact if we were able to invest in rectifying just these three issues. When she came back to me a few days later, I was frankly shocked when she reported that address changes were our biggest issue. This was our most common complaint by far by both customers and staff. This was unbelievable. I thought the top complaints would be about deposit rates being too low or overdraft fees being too high or a certain type of failed transactions, which were all high on the list, but to have address changes the single most frequent complaint was stunning.

Digging into this deeper, it turned out that to change a customer's address on the system, our employees had to go into thirteen separate legacy systems and change each one manually. This not only took a lot of time for our staff to complete, but it led to our customers staying on hold or standing in line for far too long.

Worse, the probability of an error was high. One manual entry error would affect everything, meaning our customers would have to call us again in a few weeks when the same issue arose.

Another common complaint was less surprising, and it's one I had noticed myself. I'd spent a lot of time walking down high streets to various branches with my face buried in my phone, and I'd always know I had arrived at a Barclays branch without having to look up because the dirt and grime on the building was a clear sign that I'd reached my destination.

Being a 300-year-old bank, we owned some beautiful, old buildings in prime locations in almost every town and city in England. The problem was that we hadn't done a good job of looking after these great buildings. Any capital that could be used to refurbish our estate was transferred to other divisions for purposes that were considered more important and had what they thought was a better return on investment. This was yet another contributor to the cultural degradation as investing in our personal customer and employee experience in what was essentially the "storefront window" to our brand wasn't deemed to have any value. While on the outside, they were dirty, on the inside, it only got worse.

I remember visiting one branch and going to the restroom in the basement, which was cold and damp. I shook my head as I stood there, embarrassed that this is what we had to offer our employees as an organization. And then, as I washed my hands, my jaw dropped.

We were in the basement, so the only window was a small strip overhead that looked out to an alley. They had placed a cage over this small window so people wouldn't break in, but this cage wasn't big enough to keep a pigeon out. One had managed to get trapped inside this cage, and all I could do was watch as it aimlessly flapped its wings in panic. It was dying, and my embarrassment switched to anger as I realized how beautiful our shiny, new, high rise head office in Canary Wharf was, yet our colleagues were subjected to such an awful experience.

This wasn't an isolated incident. The buildings were beautiful—the state of them was not. We refused to spend money on refurbishing them, but it was costing us so much more by refusing to act.

I share this story only to highlight that dysfunctional cultures have many far-reaching tentacles and the underlying causes can be hidden in plain sight. But these examples helped me to galvanize the team to action as they were just two examples of issues that clearly impacted morale and, therefore, performance. As I've already said a few times, we didn't need stricter management oversight and better customer service training. We needed to remove the barriers to high performance that were costing us dearly. The insight gathering phase was an absolutely crucial beginning to our transformation.

STEP TWO: ESTABLISH A COMMON LANGUAGE

Before any message of change can be delivered, it's important to make sure that there is a consistent message and that everyone is hearing the same things. To organize communications consistently and effectively, it's necessary to view the transformation through the lens of how the change benefits the employee and the customer, clearly explaining what needs to be done and why. It also needs to be done in a way that resonates with the entire company, unifying everyone's contribution. The common language that permeates all communications is the first necessary gateway that opens the way for all the subsequent steps. Taking each in turn, just as before, the impact on employees and customers needs to provide the context for any message.

With regard to the impact on employees, consider first that the communication must successfully transcend every layer of the organization and resonate with every individual, regardless of level or stature within the company. Mass mobilization is required to unify everyone to the common cause.

To do this, it's important to understand that employees first tend to view change in terms of how they will be personally impacted. Yet most companies use messaging explaining why the change will benefit the company, which creates an instant disconnect. Employees are trying to determine if the changes are a threat to their jobs, income, and career trajectory, as well as their ability to serve their customers, or if these changes help them to thrive in these areas. The empathetic leader understands this basic aspect of human nature and crafts communications that deal with this reality first before talking about the benefits to the company.

This involves understanding that the things employees most want from their jobs is that they have purpose and meaning from their work and to be able to contribute meaningfully to the overall success of the mission. In addition, they want to be recognized for their contribution and establish strong relationships with their colleagues. This knowledge helps to form the communications and is the basis for a common language that activates everyone from every layer in the company. Employees also want to grow as individuals from a knowledge and capability standpoint to assist them in achieving success. The transformation plan should be rolled out with language that helps explain what's in it for the employees, why it's a more desirable culture for the organization, and how their career objectives are more likely to be achieved. Using their own words to describe the challenges of the current situation informs the case for change and is a powerful force in aligning everyone to the cause.

The Impact on Customers:

Since almost every organization's vision includes assisting customers in some way, communications must be crafted in a way that emphasizes the benefits to the customer of the endgame, not just the things that need to be changed or eliminated. Certainly, there is a need to provide context around why the current reality is undesirable, but since energy follows focus, it's important to emphasize how the achievement of the vision looks and feels—not just to those within the organization but to the customers. The collective energy of the company must be on fulfilling the brand promise to customers and making their lives better in some way. This is crucial in building the foundation of a customer-centric organization and became the common denominator in every change we proposed. The impact to the customer became our authentic purpose, which galvanized the focus of the organization toward a new reality.

The awareness of the impact on employees and customers is then followed by establishing and communicating the organizational values as a key component of the common language. These are the things that the company stands for, the non-negotiables that guide the behaviors, and the intended impact on every constituent of the company. These values are the "true north" guiding the strategies, decisions, poli-cies, and practices that support the desired culture and drive the desired outcome. Often, a lot of work may go into cre-ating the values that best fit the organization, only to have them largely ignored in practice, which, as I've pointed out, is the early onset of a potentially dysfunctional culture and a signal to all that the stated values can be ignored because the practiced values are what really drives the company. This erodes confidence in leadership, creates distrust in manage-ment's motives, loses employee engagement, and—when the values gap becomes too large—damages the financial performance of the company. At Barclays, the discussion to set the values at the onset helped us develop the other sup-porting principles, such as adult-to-adult communications, providing transparency through context, and incorporating the customer perspective in everything we do.

STEP THREE: ADDRESS THE VITAL FEW

Begin addressing the "vital few" activities in this next phase. It's important to gain momentum by acting on some no-regrets actions, otherwise known as low-hanging fruit. Investing in refreshing and relaunching our new branch design and streamlining the address change process were two great examples that showed all our colleagues that the transformation was real.

But this is also where analyzing the product propositions and refreshing them to acknowledge the customer insights comes into play. It makes sense to prioritize the biggest issues but also the highest value segments with the most promising product refreshes. For example, during our in-home customer research, we learned that customers didn't view their savings the same way banks do. They couldn't figure out why they had to use liquid savings to get a higher interest rate than their current accounts. They didn't like having to transfer money back and forth to be able to pay bills while maximizing their yield on their money. Their question was why the bank couldn't develop an all-in-one account, so they didn't have to think about their liquid funds all the time. So, we developed essentially a money market account—but with far more convenience features—that was incredibly well-received. We made product amendments to mortgages and personal loans to reflect insights from customers and staff, as well.

We were able to make quick-hit systems and process improvements that helped employees do their jobs better and more easily than before. This provided validation in the eyes of the employees that management had heard the employee feedback and were acting on it in the short term while laying the groundwork for bigger, long-term plans.

STEP FOUR: CREATE A TRANSFORMATION JOURNEY

The fourth phase of the transformation journey is to create a physical representation or roadmap of the journey. We found this to be extremely useful in depicting the collective process, and it was a valuable reference point for upcoming changes. Many leaders believe that this is the only thing needed to transform their culture, but it's just one—albeit important—piece.

The map needs to begin by providing detail on the current reality and building the case for change. In our case, we showed this portion of the map in the upper left-hand corner, complete with data to support the case for change, citing the *Whistleblower* program and the feedback from customer and employee focus groups. The point was to use this as the baseline for the transformation program and to underscore the severity of the challenge—the need to change was urgent and non-negotiable.

In the upper right hand of the map was the desired future state. This is where we depicted the six stakeholders or constituents–Customers, Colleagues, Capital Markets, Communities, Regulators, and Union–and what a successful fulfillment of the transformation would mean to each, complete with the aspirational metrics I described earlier. This "future reality" activated the group mindset that there were massive benefits to every stakeholder by successfully fulfilling the vision and demonstrated that our singular focus on shareholders had to shift to achieve those aspirations. These stretch goals were instrumental in shifting our collective mindset as we had to stop settling for attempting to hit plan or making small, incremental improvements on historical underperformance.

The message here was clear: We will meet and exceed the needs of *all* constituents in ways that have far greater impact. We will not allow one group (i.e., shareholders) to dominate the focus. And, even more important, we would not accept tradeoffs—underperforming on one outcome to boost another. For example, we would not sacrifice financial performance to improve the customer experience.

This was not a typical mindset at all in the organization at the time. Before our transformational journey, the dominating belief was that we desperately had to hit our financial targets and accept tradeoffs in service, investment in the infrastructure, and systems enhancements as a necessary consequence. Shifting this mindset laid the foundation of our balanced scorecard: Customer metrics, Colleague metrics, Management metrics (efficiency and productivity gains), Risk and Compliance metrics, and Financial metrics. The overarching message was to send the very clear message that we would outperform across *every* dimension of our scorecard, exceeding the expectations of *all* constituents. And we did, in stunning fashion.

STEP FIVE: SET YOUR BUSINESS PLAN AND STRETCH ASPIRATIONS

The top part of the map, as a banner connecting the current reality on the left to the future outcome on the right, should contain the vision statement, which should be a unique statement on our aspiration. The vision statement is saying what an organization will do. Instead of saying we would be the best bank in the UK, like every other bank in the UK, there was no reason that we couldn't be the best bank in the world. The point was to shift our thinking from "How could we possibly do that when we have a big enough challenge just trying to climb out of the hole we're in?" to "Why not us? Someone has to be the best bank in the world and that should be us."

As you can imagine, there was plenty of resistance. Many of the senior leaders were bound by "realistic" objectives. The challenge with realistic objectives is that, first they're subjective, and second, they create a false, self-limiting ceiling put into place to manage expectations and avoid disappointment. But this flies in the face of our confidence that we had a world-class leadership team. If we were all truly world class leaders, then the organization's performance should surely reflect that, and we should be benchmarking ourselves to the top banks in the world. Period. Confidence is contagious and we had to project absolute confidence that we had the team, the resources, and the assets to be the best in order to change the belief system of a fairly downtrodden organization.

Now this may seem like a straightforward point, but it was an incredibly important part of the process as, remember, the aim was to change the entire ecosystem and part of this was to ignite passion for the journey to come and to reinforce that the destination made it all worthwhile.

The mission statement, which is the statement that describes the organization's purpose for being, was written underneath the vision and served to connect the current reality on the left with the desired future reality on the right. These statements should then be supported by the list of corporate values. This banner across the top serves as a visual reminder of the common purpose that unites the organization and the behaviors you commit to honor.

This is where many program managers stop, thinking the journey has now been laid out, but there are some other important components to include. This map is a living document of change and growth. These components represent the body of the map, which contains the whole of the plan to transform the organization, meaning the priorities and the work that needs to be done. The best way to approach this is to organize the various activities under key themes to allow for simultaneous progress by the various teams that support the outcome. In our case, our ace COO spent two days with the executive team developing this comprehensive plan, prioritizing each key action based on considerations of budget, impact, and ease of completion. We then put these activities under five themes, which were:

Customer Propositions: Refreshing every product offering, viewed through the lens of delivering better customer outcomes.

Employee Value Propositions: Reviewing rewards and incentives to support our new value system, overhauling the performance management systems and training designed to upskill all colleagues.

Improve Channels: Changing the reporting lines in the organizational structure to reflect a focus on customers over products and launch major investment in the channels—physical, telephony, and digital—to improve the customer and employee experience.

Improve Processes: Making banking easier for customers by making the work easier for employees, launching Lean workstreams for process improvements, improving customer applications, ease of onboarding across every product line, and improving post-sale follow-ups with customers to ensure their understanding of the product features and terms.

Performance Improvement Metrics: Creating the baseline metrics for measuring performance across the five score-card dimensions and tracking and communicating results regularly.

These five pillars supported the more granular plan depicted in the body of the map. Every time there was a change, we would communicate this to all employees by showing where on the map the work fit, helping to provide context, clarity, and the rationale for each change. It was also a good morale boost as it showed that the promised investment in over-hauling the organization continued.

This was beneficial because we were also asking our employees to change quite a bit, and we needed them to invest their time and energy into learning new information and apply-ing this information in new ways. We were asking much more of our first-line managers. Securing their belief that they played a crucial role in our ability to change in ways that were impactful to their customers, as well as creating confidence that outstanding performance on their parts would lead to higher pay and career advancement, was the fuel that made the transformation possible.

Having every employee feel that the cultural transforma-tion for Barclays was also their personal transformation was magical. If organizations spend incredible time and energy on product propositions for their customers, they need to do the same for their employees. For us, there was the need for considerable training to help each person develop greater skills working in an environment where they were empow-ered to run their business with accountability.

This was what created discretionary energy—having full engagement in the changes.

The map was an important visual aide to help define and track the journey, but the narrative—which is used to connect all the insights, plan components, and leadership with the rest of the company—was equally important. We conducted major launches in every market, explaining every detail of the map with stories to provide context for each step and create an emotional connection to the outcome. And we led every meeting off with excerpts from the *Whistleblower* program. This took the air out of the room and reminded everyone in attendance that we needed to change and change fast. There is no better way to do this than to share insights from the very people in those meetings as the impetus for the change along with examples of the behaviors that supported the new culture. Letting the employees in the room know that they had been heard and that their ideas helped to frame the change created palpable energy.

It also announced a new role for management, which was demonstrated in the narrative, that we were committed to doing more than monitoring behaviors and performance. Leadership's role was to create an environment that allowed every employee the chance to succeed, which created an alignment and connection that didn't exist before. The stories told in the rollout were kept alive in the subsequent communications as the program advanced. Everyone could see what was changing and why. The fact that the Employee Value Proposition work resulted in more promotions from within showed true commitment. It supported the understanding that there was a reward for the highest-performing employees, creating career movement that wasn't always the case before.

The narrative must come alive and resonate with each person. Many companies have attempted to transform their culture by creating a map of a journey but make the narrative all about how the employees need to adapt to a new normal and behave differently. This is not going to inspire any discretionary effort by employees as leadership practices remain intact. Therefore, it does nothing to change the culture. But when it's prefaced by management listening and incorporating the employee's feedback in the design, the effect is incredibly dramatic, and the soul of the company is rediscovered.

REFLECTIVE EXERCISE

1. What insight and analytics need to be understood in order to build a high-performing culture?

_____

_____

_____

_____

_____

_____

_____

_____

_____

_____

_____

2. What organizational "common language" needs to be accepted by all to build a high-performance culture?

_____

_____

_____

_____

_____

_____

_____

3. What low-hanging fruit can immediately be harvested to see immediate result of this new high-performance culture?

_____

_____

_____

_____

_____

_____

4. What does your transformation journey look like in the form of a physical roadmap or business plan?

_____

_____

_____

_____

_____

_____

5. What needs to be done to get started on the implementation of your new high-performance cultural plan?

_____

_____

_____

_____

_____

_____

_____

_____

_____

_____

_____

_____

_____

_____

SUMMARY/KEY TAKEAWAYS

One of the most important aspects of a cultural transformation is to understand the impact that any changes have on employees and customers. By organizing the transformation program through this lens, a leader can create a map of the intended journey from today's reality to the desired future state. Using employees and customers' insights as fuel for the journey, this map clearly sets out the challenges that currently exist and the rewards when the vision is accomplished. This framework is crucial as it allows for a structured message of change that is consistent and organized so that everyone is hearing the same things. No one is exempt from this change, and it requires everyone's buy-in. It's a valuable communication tool at the onset, but also during the journey to provide context for any changes and to measure the progress.

21

FOCUSING ON PEOPLE AND LEADERSHIP

"If your actions inspire others to dream more, learn more,
do more and become more, you are a leader."
– John Adams

This approach will produce exceptional results in any geography and any line of business. In the process of unlocking the latent performance in an organization, combined with the philosophies I've shared for each step in the journey, the core role and relevance of management is redefined. The current role of management as a control function is so deeply ingrained that to shift to being responsible for creating an environment that brings the highest performance across all dimensions of the scorecard—rather than simply managing the numbers—can be incredibly counterintuitive and difficult to fully embrace.

But the results of this case study are undeniable. The UK Retail Bank, once seen as the weakest part of the Barclays franchise, took its rightful place as the crown jewel of the whole organization. The singular focus on Profit and Loss was replaced by a new and more powerful definition of P&L

to mean "People and Leadership." This necessitated treating profits as the outcome of success, which paradoxically resulted in higher profits. My goal for sharing this experience and incredible outcome is to help business owners, leaders, and those within a management structure understand that putting people first—while aligning the values of the individuals and organization—drives significant shareholder value through improved performance, increased employee engagement, a systemically diverse and inclusive culture, and succession planning that rewards the best and brightest talent. For people to be seen as the most important resource in an organization, they must be developed, valued, and invested in—just like any other asset. The sense of entitlement many companies have toward their workforce must be replaced with a deeper appreciation for the value of improved performance and the pathway to unlocking this value.

Following the success in the UK, we were able to expand Real Retail to Europe, Africa, and the emerging markets in the form of Customer Plans that incorporated the transformation process we had developed in the UK. These plans reflected the process of gathering insights, developing products with unique customer value propositions, and an employee value proposition that created an environment where discretionary energy unleashed higher performance.

That phone call from the BBC was easily the most traumatic experience in my professional life. As often happens with significant events like that, whether positive or negative, it turned into the greatest gift we could ever have received, even though the pressure to avoid any missteps and rapidly display improved performance was intense. The cultural transformation that resulted was an incredible experience for all involved, and no one was left unchanged.

As I mentioned at the onset, I decided to not share any names because it would mean that no matter how many people I recognized, there would be some left out. Obviously, this information on transforming the culture of a large organization was a massive team effort, and it took the contribution of many key leaders to learn alongside me how to land the transformation with such dramatic success. They were also patient with me as my way of viewing business and leadership is certainly not conventional.

I knew that there is indeed a better way to win. Now you do, too.

CONCLUDING THOUGHTS

PRODUCING EXCEPTIONAL RESULTS

"If you focus on results, you will never change.
If you focus on change, you will get results."
– Jack Dixon, PHD, Distinguished Professor,
UCSD School of Medicine

Now that you've read this book, the question I have is "Now what?" Now that you can see that creating an intentional culture aligned to values that authentically inform the vision and strategy of an organization creates highly engaged employees who routinely outperform expectations, how will you apply parts (or all) of these insights to your organization? To your career? How can you bring these strategies to life to realize tangible benefits?

REFLECTIVE EXERCISE

1. I would like to challenge you with an assignment to begin considering how you can do this: Knowing where you, or your organization, are today, write down where you wish it

(or you) were. In other words, what is your destination? So often, we think about what things about today's reality we don't want, but this is your chance to identify what you do want. Then write down who benefits from you achieving that destination.

_____

_____

_____

_____

_____

_____

_____

_____

_____

_____

_____

_____

_____

_____

_____

_____

_____

_____

_____

_____

_____

_____

2. In the lines below, write out a dozen new actions that you will take immediately and implement within the next ninety days to put your organization on track to achieve a

better way to win. In essence, this becomes your executive summary of your business plan or playbook to achieve and produce exceptional results:

1. _____

2. _____

3. _____

4. _____

5. _____

6. _____

7. _____

8. _____

9. _____

10. _____

11. _____

12. _____

Through the experiences I have shared in this book, you know that the crisis we faced was the fuel to create the transformational program necessary to build a functional organization, based on a powerful vision of what a high-performing organization would look like, with all the subsequent benefits that come with that. Starting with this one small step begins the same process for you and your organization. Whether I'm advising a multi-billion-dollar organization, a divisional team, or a small startup, the initial step is always the same.

Knowing the destination that awaits your organization or team at the end of the journey is incredibly motivating, and I encourage you to reach out to me so that we can turn this motivation into the inspiration necessary to build your transformational plan that will fuel the journey to a higher-performing—much higher-performing—organization.

I'm equally interested in speaking to anyone wanting to take the step in their career about my personal mentoring program, which will guide you to perform at higher levels in your existing role, whether you're a CEO or not, or light the path to advancing your career one or even two levels. This proven program helps set you up for incredible success. Reach out and talk to me about your personal circumstances in a complimentary introductory session and I'll gladly share more specifics.

You can contact me at mikeamato@amatosparks.com or (425) 922-8086. You are certainly welcome to email me, but due to spam blockers, I prefer that you text me direct to ensure that I receive your query.

Kindly,

ABOUT THE AUTHOR

MIKE AMATO is an author, professional speaker, executive leadership business coach and consultant, and owner of a Ambassador Wines in Washington State. He began his career in financial services by answering the phones as a temporary telephone representative at Washington Mutual, a small savings bank with fifty-four branches. Over the next twenty-four years, Mike's career growth paralleled that of the bank when he was named President of the Retail Bank with over 2,100 branches, overseeing aggressive growth via the acquisition of more than thirty banks and opening new branches in new markets around the country.

When the culture of the organization began to shift with new leadership guiding a dramatic expansion of subprime lending, Mike left Washington Mutual and relocated to London for Barclays Bank as Head of Global Product and Distribution with over 3,100 branches worldwide. At the time, Barclays was an underperforming organization, and he was tasked with launching one of the largest banking transformations in UK banking history, with significant, measurable performance uplifts across every dimension of the balanced scorecard. This was done by focusing primarily on boosting employee engagement scores from worst in the UK to the top bank globally, while developing customer-centric products and services that moved customer advocacy to the top in the UK.

Following his executive career, Mike joined the board of directors at Santander UK and as senior independent director at Tandem Bank, a digital banking startup in London. Mike was chair of the Nominations and Remunerations Committee, where he oversaw the strategic alignment process designed to connect the vision, mission, strategy, and subsequent business plan in ways that were consistent with the values of the organization.

Today, Mike is a much sought-after keynote speaker and advisor, helping organizations transform to much higher performance by focusing on people over profits. He also is a mentor and career guide to executive and senior managers desiring to grow their performance, influence, and careers to new heights. In addition to this, Mike is an owner of Ambassador Wines, an award-winning winery in Washington state and just named as one of the top 100 wineries in the world.

ABOUT MIKE AMATO'S EXECUTIVE BUSINESS COACHING AND ADVISORY SERVICES

Mike Amato has helped business leaders and executive management teams all over the world achieve outstanding success.

If you want to stand out from your competition, strengthen your credentials, and fix dysfunction…then finding your better way to win is paramount.

Mike will help you crack the code to enhancing your influence in your current role or to taking the next step—or two—up the career ladder, unlocking your potential impact with stunning results.

Helping you to understand how to magnify the many strengths that helped you get to where you are today, while creating awareness of the things that can work against you and derail your effectiveness, Mike will show you how to improve your leadership reach, stakeholder management, and situational awareness in ways that announce your candidacy for the next levels.

Your program will be uniquely tailored to you, no matter what your level in the organization, whether business owner, CEO, executive manager, or team leader. You will be amazed at how your impact on the business improves, as well as by the other aspects of your life that will be enhanced by your success.

If you are a leader who desires to transform the performance of your organization or team, whether it's driven by a crisis, chronic underperformance, or lacking innovation and energy, contact Mike to discuss how to completely transform the collective energy, and subsequently the output, of your team.

Through a process of strategic alignment, Mike will create a bespoke transformation program for you that will bring your vision to life and lead to outperforming every key performance indicator. He will teach you how to create a culture where everyone is driven by discretionary energy and renewed dedication to the purpose. You will see—and feel—the difference in a surprisingly short period of time.

For more information, visit Mike's website listed below and then text him with your name, time zone, and the best time to redeem a 30-60 minute, no-obligation business consultation by phone or Zoom.

MikeAmato@AmatoSparks.com
www.AmatoSparks.com
(425) 922-8086

ABOUT AMBASSADOR WINES OF WASHINGTON

In 2005, Mike and his co-founders planted twenty-six acres of Bordeaux and Rhone varietals in the internationally renowned Red Mountain AVA in Washington State. Committed to creating a world class vineyard and winery operation, the team set out to attract the very best vineyard management and winemaking talent to bring their vision to life.

Today, producing just 3,000 cases of wine in their boutique operation, Ambassador Wines has won numerous industry and wine critic awards, culminating in being named one of the Top-100 wineries in the world by *Wine and Spirits Magazine*. Their success has stemmed from creating a culture that highlights excellence in all areas of the Three Ts: Terroir, Talent, and Taste. With the strong belief that life is too short to drink anything but the best wines, each wine is thoughtfully blended, artfully balanced, and bold yet restrained.

As Mike always says, "We're very data driven, and our data shows that 100 percent of our customers are happier after drinking our wine." So, contact Mike to make an appointment to visit one of their two tasting rooms in Woodinville,

Washington, or place an order online to experience these stunning wines firsthand and, well, be happy!

MikeAmato@AmatoSparks.com
www.AmbassadoryWinery.com